KT-393-306

WITHDRAWN FROM
THE LIBRARY

UNIVERSITY OF
WINCHESTER

.EGE
R 2004

Dance Technology:

Current Applications and Future Trends

Judith A. Gray, ed.

Sponsored by the
National Dance Association
an association of the
American Alliance for Health, Physical
Education, Recreation, and Dance

KA 0209092 9

Cover slide by Ted Pope, University of Wisconsin

KING ALFRED'S COLLEGE
WINCHESTER

02090929

Copyright ©1989
The American Alliance for Health, Physical
Education, Recreation, and Dance
1900 Association Drive
Reston, Virginia 22091
ISBN 0-88314-429-8

I wish to dedicate this book to my colleagues in the National Dance Association and especially to those who helped establish the new field of dance technology. My special thanks go to Gordy Stephenson, Buff Brennan, Dede Petty, Margot Apostolos, and Ted Pope who have been with me in this endeavor from the very beginning. Finally, I would like to gratefully acknowledge the data entry effort of Lea Weaver and the copy editing of Ellen Meyer.

Purposes of the American Alliance for Health, Physical Education, Recreation, and Dance

The American Alliance is an educational organization, structured for the purposes of supporting, encouraging, and providing assistance to member groups and their personnel throughout the nation as they seek to initiate, develop, and conduct programs in health, leisure, and movement-related activities for the enrichment of human life.

Alliance objectives include:

1. Professional growth and development—to support, encourage, and provide guidance in the development and conduct of programs in health, leisure, and movement-related activities which are based on the needs, interests, and inherent capacities of the individual in today's society.

2. Communication—to facilitate public and professional understanding and appreciation of the importance and value of health, leisure, and movement-related activities as they contribute toward human well-being.

3. Research—to encourage and facilitate research which will enrich the depth and scope of health, leisure, and movement-related activities; and to disseminate the findings to the profession and other interested and concerned publics.

4. Standards and guidelines—to further the continuous development and evaluation of standards within the profession for personnel and programs in health, leisure, and movement-related activities.

5. Public affairs—to coordinate and administer a planned program of professional, public, and governmental relations that will improve education in areas of health, leisure, and movement-related activities.

6. To conduct such other activities as shall be approved by the Board of Governors and the Alliance Assembly, provided that the Alliance shall not engage in any activity which would be inconsistent with the status of an educational and charitable organization as defined in Section 501(c)(3) of the Internal Revenue Code of 1954 or any successor provision thereto, and none of the said purposes shall at any time be deemed or construed to be purposes other than the public benefit purposes and objectives consistent with such educational and charitable status.

Bylaws, Article III

Foreword

It is always exciting to witness the emergence of a new branch of research, and with this book edited by Dr. Judith Gray, we have that rare opportunity. *Dance Technology: Current Applications and Future Trends* is the first assemblage of original research in this new hybrid field joining the arts and the sciences. This book, a milestone in dance publications, is an eye-opener for the arts world as well as the computer field. The National Dance Association has been supportive of the efforts of Dr. Gray and her fellow researchers.

The National Dance Association was extremely visionary in their support of this new branch of dance research by sponsoring the first symposium on dance technology, coordinated by Dr. Gray, at Anaheim, California in 1984, when there were only a handful of researchers. By 1986, when they sponsored the second symposium, held in Cincinnati, Ohio, the number of researchers had doubled. Now there is a broad international network of dance technology researchers. Authors and researchers from the United States, Canada and Australia share the results of their efforts in such diverse areas as image digitizing, robot choreography, movement analysis, databases for dance, computerized dance notation, and computerized lightboards to be used in dance performance.

Dance and technology make seemingly odd partners. Dance is the most ethereal of art forms and computer technology perhaps the most concrete of sciences. Whereas technologists deal with the logical, the scientifically verifiable, dancers, as artists, deal with the illogical, i.e. inspiration and finding truth in that which cannot be spoken. Although dancers may be overcoming their "computer anxiety," still the research and innovations in technology seem remote or even contrary to the dancers' quest to create art, an activity often shrouded in mystique. Thinking that computers were only useful as number crunchers or word processors, initially many choreographers were reluctant to interact with such impersonal objects in such a personal endeavor as choreography. Choreography is held sacred by many as a personal statement made by an artist to communicate to an audience. What place could computers have in such an individualistic and initially private endeavor?

And on the other side of this new partnership, those not conversant in the language of dance, which often is communicated only with difficulty through words, found dance an impenetrable subject. Yet represented here are the pioneers who have bridged the gap between art and science, dance and computers, to find mutual support and interest. Each of the authors came to their research from different points of view as dance performers, teachers, choreographers, and computer scientists, to find new applications for computer technology, better ways to analyze movement and dance technique, to create and record their choreography and theories of dance technique.

Therefore, the studies in this anthology vary in their orientation to the subject and in sophistication representing the broad scope of research presently being conducted in dance technology. Because of the variety presented here, each reader will be able to find their own entree into the field. Whether you have only a beginning interest in either computers or dance, or already have a sophisticated knowledge base from which to draw, you will be able to find in the articles presented here something to pique your interest. For the dancers there are new ideas to spark the creative urge and methodologies to use in the classroom. For the computer scientist there are also new ideas to develop further research and new applications of computer technology.

Dianne Howe
Assistant Professor in Dance
University of California, Irvine
Past President, National Dance Association, 1989

Author Information

JUDITH A. GRAY, Ph.D.: Former assistant professor of Dance at the University of Wisconsin, Madison, Judith Gray earned her doctorate at the University of Arizona in 1978. She has since served as senior lecturer in the Department of Theater and Dance at California Polytechnic State University, and recently spent a year in New Zealand teaching, writing, and lecturing. She has worked with computers extensively in the areas of dance teacher behavior recording, data analysis, image digitizing, and desktop publishing. Her articles on dance technology and dance education have appeared in several professional journals, including *Quest*, *Dance Research Journal*, *Design for Arts in Education*, *British Journal of Educational Studies*, and *JOHPERD*.

MARY A. BRENNAN, Ph.D.: "Buff" Brennan is an associate professor and recent coordinator of the dance program at the University of Wisconsin-Madison. She began her research on computerizing movement analysis in the early 1980s, and has since developed a highly efficient and error-free methodology for determining movement profiles. Dr. Brennan has published in several professional journals, including the *Research Quarterly for Exercise and Sport*, and was responsible for the compilation of *Dance Research III*. In 1986, her contributions to the dance profession were acknowledged when she received the National Dance Association Scholar award.

ALICE TREXLER, Ph.D.:Alice Trexler is currently a choreographer in Boston and director of the Tufts University Dance Program. She has taught at Wellesley, Bryn Mawr, and NYU. She received her doctorate from NYU in 1976 and her master's degree from Columbia Teachers' College. Her major interests are in improvisational and experimental approaches to dance and her work in computerized motion detection with Ronald Thornton is an extension of this interest. She has presented papers at several national conferences, including the 1986 Arts and Technology Symposium at Connecticut College.

RONALD K. THORNTON, Ph.D.: Ronald K. Thornton is a physicist who is director of Research and Development at the Center for Science and Math Teaching at Tufts University, and a project associate at Technical Education Research Centers (TERC). He is also director of Tools for Scientific Thinking, a national project funded by FIPSE (U.S. Dept. of Education). The project intends to involve college students in science and to develop their physical intuition using microcomputer-based laboratory tools of the type used in earlier performances.

MARGO APOSTOLOS, Ph.D.: Margo Apostolos is currently the director of the dance program at the University of Southern California in Los Angeles. She recently received her Ph.D. from Stanford University where she first developed her unique dance research area in robotics, incorporating both technological and philosophic approaches to robotic movement.

Her work has been seen on television and she has presented papers at national conventions, including the National Dance Association Dance and Computers Symposium in 1985, the International Computers in Engineering Conference and Exhibition in 1985, and the American Society of Mechanical Engineers in 1986. Her papers have appeared in the Proceedings of several conferences, including the IEEE International Conference on Robotics and Automation, and the 5th Annual Microcomputers in Education Conference.

DIANNA PETTY, MFA: Dianna Petty is currently completing her second degree at UCLA. One degree has an emphasis on choreography and performance and is from the Dance Department, while the other degree is from the UCLA Theater Arts-Producers Program and has an emphasis on Dance Management. Her work on "Absolute (0.0.0.)" was in partial completion towards the Dance degree. Upon graduation, Dianna plans to continue working with computer graphics and choreography and hopes to develop animated sequences of movement. She is now doing an internship at the Los Angeles Music Center Education Division, experiencing administration and management responsibilities for nonprofit arts organizations.

NORMAN BADLER, Ph.D.: Dr. Norman Badler is a professor in the Department of Computer and Information Science at the University of Pennsylvania. He received his Ph.D. degree in Computer Science in 1975 from the University of Toronto, and has authored or co-authored over 50 scientific papers.

THOMAS W. CALVERT, Ph.D.: Thomas W. Calvert is a professor of kinesiology and computing science at Simon Fraser University. He holds a bachelor degree from University College, London, a master's degree from Wayne State University, and a Ph.D. from Carnegie Mellon University. He is widely published in both computer and dance journals.

STANLEY D. KAHN: As a dancer, Stanley Kahn appeared in many San Francisco area productions in all dance forms—ballet, tap, and acrobatics—culminating in a vaudeville engagement with Joe Laurie, Jr. He has taught and choreographed in New York, Oklahoma, and San Francisco, and after World War II, he opened the Mason-Kahn Studios in San Francisco. His tap dance notation system has been copyrighted under the name "Kahnotation," and is now being adapted to the Macintosh computer.

RHONDA RYMAN: Rhonda Ryman is an associate professor of dance at the University of Waterloo, Ontario, Canada, where she conducts research at the University's Computer Graphics Laboratory. She has presented papers at national conferences and appears in several Proceedings.

PAULA DOZZI: Paula Dozzi is a graduate student in dance and kinesiology at the University of Waterloo, Ontario, Canada.

GEORGE POLITIS, Ph.D.: George Politis conducts his dance technology research in Benesh notation in the Baser Department of Computer Science at the University of Sydney, Sydney, Australia.

Table Of Contents

Tables and Figures

Chapter 7
A COMPUTERIZED PROCEDURE FOR RECORDING AND ANALYZING DANCE TEACHER MOBILITY

Chapter 8
A COMPUTER PROGRAM FOR THE ENTRY OF BENESH NOTATION

Chapter 9
A COMPUTER-ASSISTED INVESTIGATION INTO THE EFFECTS OF HEEL CONTACT IN BALLET ALLEGRO

Chapter 10
A COMPUTERIZED METHODOLOGY USING LABAN MOVEMENT ANALYSIS TO DETERMINE MOVEMENT PROFILES IN DANCE

Chapter 11
THE COMPUTERIZED PRODUCTION OF EDUCATIONAL MATERIAL ON
BENESH MOVEMENT NOTATION

Chapter 12
ABSOLUTE (0,0,0): DANCE INFLUENCED BY TECHNOLOGICAL
ENVIRONMENTS AND COMPUTERS

Chapter 13
CAPTURING AND PROCESSING DANCE IMAGES WITH COMPUTERS

Chapter 14
COMPUTERIZED LIGHTING DESIGN FOR DANCE : AN INTERVIEW WITH
DAVID ELLIOT

Chapter 15
THE UNIVERSITY'S ROLE IN THE FUTURE OF DANCE TECHNOLOGY

1 The Evolution of Dance Technology

Judith A. Gray
San Francisco State University
San Francisco, California.

Art expands human conscience and sensitivity. Technology expands human power. The history of technology is punctuated by noteworthy inventions and scientific breakthroughs which have greatly influenced the events of our history. The arts on the other hand, have sought to reflect and idealize the course of history. The arts and technology have coexisted for centuries, and over the years the arts have been affected in various degrees by machines and tools. Notwithstanding, today's technology is a force unto itself and is unlike any other machinery or tool invented and developed heretofore.

Figure 1.1
Dance: The art of human movement.

Of all the arts, dance would seem the least likely to accede to the vagaries of rapid change and the relentless advances of this modern technology. Dance, the art of human movement, on the surface appears nontechnologically inclined. It is the self-sufficient art. Indeed, dance education pioneer Margaret H'Doubler believed that dancers were their own teachers, students, textbooks, and laboratories. She would have no doubt included computers in that list had she been aware of their existence and function. Despite her claims, which are still echoed throughout the profession, during the past decade in particular, on university campuses and in dance studios both here and abroad, a small group of dance researchers, choreographers, and educators has astounded the dance field by demonstrating their proficiency and creativity with computer technology.

This group, representing the cutting edge of dance research, has been steadily growing, convening, and corresponding and has subsequently formed themselves into a new and daring branch of the dance discipline—Dance Technology. Several of them are represented in this book and the technologies they predominantly employ are computers, robots, and electronics. To understand the impact this research is having on dance and to provide a basis for future predictions, let us first take a look at the brief, yet significant history of the influence of dance technology in our lives and work.

Dance Notation

The first attempts to consider the possible collaboration between computers and dance occurred in the 1960s at the University of Pittsburgh. Under the direction of Jean Beaman, the choreographic process was gingerly codified and manipulated using a computer and a comparatively remarkable memory capacity—although sadly, the results of this collaboration were neither published nor performed. In the 1970s a few dance researchers devised a methodology to computerize Labanotation—the symbolic "scoring" system for coding and recording dances. David Sealy at Iowa University later streamlined these efforts and produced a series of computer programs for Labanotation which were able to edit, format, analyze, scan, and manipulate dance scores that had been entered into his system by means of a unique IBM selectric keyboard containing only Laban symbols. It wasn't long before computerized dance notation systems incorporated graphics and sound so that notated dances could be reproduced symbolically on a monitor along with synthesized sound effects.

Meanwhile, other dance notation systems were following suit. At the University of Sydney in Australia and at the University of Waterloo in Canada dance researchers computerized the Benesh dance notation system. The logical consequence of efficient recording systems for dance is to experiment with transposing the movement and position symbols into human body models, preferably ones that can move.

Body Modelling for Dance

After creating and testing two-dimensional stick figures, Lynne Weber and S.W.Smoliar at Simon Fraser University produced an ellisoid body model for dance which they named "Sausage man." Although it was three-dimensional, it lacked a versatile movement range. Meanwhile, in England at the Royal College of Art, Colin Emmett had developed a body model comprised of spheres which was modestly animated, but more importantly it was able to cast shadows. This innovation enabled dance researchers to program visually more realistic joint articulations and body elevations. This body model was aptly named "Bubble man."

Experiments continued with computer animated dance figures until 1983 when at the New York Institute of Technology, Rebecca Allen designed an exquisite, lithesome computerized dancer for Twyla Tharp's video choreography titled "Catherine Wheel." Since then, much

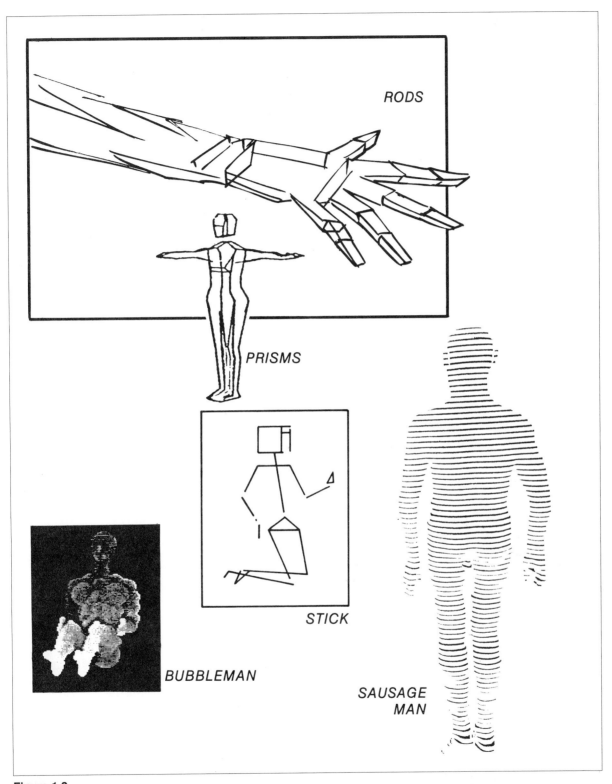

RODS

PRISMS

STICK

BUBBLEMAN

SAUSAGE
MAN

Figure 1.2
Body models for dance.

interest has been drawn to the Figure Animation Project in progress at Simon Fraser University. The goal of this project is to develop a level of motion description for articulated, humanoid figures which can be used by choreographers. This research has already resulted in lively computer graphics depicting several body models moving in preordained patterns on the monitor—an unimaginable feat only ten years ago.

Computer Choreography

Computerized dance notation systems and animated body modelling techniques have led to experiments in computer choreography. These have enjoyed qualified success. Dianne Petty at UCLA created a model of a dancer on the Geometric Design Processor—an interactive graphic system for modelling three-dimensional objects. She first photographed a series of computer-generated poses and subsequently coordinated these images with music, lighting, and live choreography to produce a unique dance performance. A more detailed description of her project is presented later in this book.

At Tufts University, a motion detector already in use in science laboratories there, has been adapted for use in dance performance experiments. Alice Trexler.and Ronald Thornton, working with dance composition students, have produced computer-generated graphs of movement paths and patterns which, they contend, will not only facilitate cross-disciplinary collaborations on campus, but will also act as aesthetic calalysts for choreographers. A chapter on these efforts has been included.

By far the most notable and dramatic application of computer expertise to choreographic intent and imagination is in the area of robotics. While completing her doctorate at Stanford University, Margot Apostolos found that the users' attitudes towards robotic aids were enhanced if they were made aware of the range of aesthetic movement qualities and possibilities. She then developed a body of work in robot choreography which stands alone as an art form. Her research in this field will be described by her later. Apostolos ably demonstrates the computer's powerful ubiquity and its expressive potential.

Dance Education Technology

Unlike other curricular areas, the dance discipline has made limited incursions into the education technology arena. At the turn of the decade, dance educators became intrigued and then briefly captivated by the potential of computerization. Attempts were made to construct CAI programs for dance in the areas of dance composition and skill aquisition. The most significant contributions were made by two dance technologists at the University of Wisconsin-Madison. Working out of the Dance Program in collaboration with computer scientists and zoologist Gordon Stephenson, Dr. Buff Brennan developed a computer-assisted methodology for analyzing dance movement, and Dr. Judith Gray designed and built a computer-based system for recording and analyzing dance teacher and learner behaviors. Both their papers can be found in this book. An interesting offshoot of Dr. Gray's work was a procedure which recorded and graphed the mobility patterns and behaviors of teachers, analyzing them in terms of rate, direction, and proximity. It has since been adapted for regular classroom use.

Databases

Somewhat related to dance education software are the database management systems which are being created to serve dance teachers, researchers, and administrators. Pat Rowe, chair of the Dance Department at New York University, and Nancy Ruyter at the University of California-Irvine, are both assembling valuable bibliographic and resource databases for dance. Also, there are presently dancer profiles and placement services for dancers which match companies looking for dancers with available and suitable performers.

Conclusion

Technology has historically affected the dance art product and the art-making process. The computer has already demonstrated a powerful role in this development and will continue to do so. However, its power will be increasingly defined in terms of artistic freedom. Information technology in particular, has the ability to free men and women from tasks that are normally difficult, dangerous, or tedious, thus allowing them to live and work more creatively.

In the following chapters readers will find examples of ongoing research and development in a variety of computer applications related to the study of dance. Since dance technology is an evolving field and a very young field, it should come as no surprise that even as this book is rolling off the presses, some applications have blossomed into more proficient techniques and others have been abandoned or replaced. Notwithstanding, the purpose of selecting these articles is to bring readers up to date with what is going on in the field. It is the first compilation of research in dance technology of its kind. Hence, its value and importance must be regarded in this light. Hopefully this book will enlighten those who desire to straddle the cutting edge of art and science and at the same time will encourage others to explore the world of computer technology as it relates to their own artistic endeavours.

2 Toward A Language For Human Movement*

Thomas W. Calvert
Simon Fraser University
Burnaby, British Columbia
Canada

The ultimate objective of this work is a language for the specification and animation of human movement. It should be interpretable by both computer and man, and while it should be applicable to movement in general, it should meet the particular needs of dance, film, and theatre. Interdisciplinary in nature, this work draws most heavily on linguistics, computer science, and kinesiology, as well as dance, film, and theatre. This paper will be limited to presentation of the theoretical basis for language and a discussion of some very limited results. The ultimate goals require substantial theoretical and practical development.

At this time, no comprehensive language for human movement exists, and for many the need for such a language may not be so obvious. Our culture is largely movement-illiterate: dance for example, has been discribed as an illiterate art. We are accustomed to rather loose descriptions of human movement, particularly day-to-day activities, and we generally do not have the vocabulary or the discipline to describe it precisely. The need for more accurate terms has recently come into focus in filmmaking, where the traditional scripts and storyboards were found to be inadequate. Earlier in the field of dance, a need to record choreography for posterity had been recognized for many years. The wide variety of notation systems developed for this purpose represent movement at a very low level. Their notation systems, however, are typically elemental, complex in details but lacking in structure (i.e., syntax). Very difficult to learn, they consequently are limited in their use. Nevertheless, experience gained through working with notation is valuable in developing an understanding of the needs for a higher level language.

Movement Specification: Notation and Storyboards

Notation Systems
In psychosocial processes, a notation system to describe movement has been developed by Scheflen (1974), and Birdwhistell (1970) has developed a complex system to describe the movements used in interpersonal communication. For general application, however, of these and other special purpose systems, only three are in common use: Benesh Notation (Benesh and Benesh, 1956), Eshkol-Wachmann Notation (Eshkol and Wachmann, 1958) and

*©1986. From *Computers and the Humanities*, Vol. 20, pp. 35–43. Reprinted by permission of Kluwer Academic Publishers.

Labanotation (Hutchinson, 1960). All three have been used to record dance, Benesh being the most popular in the U.K. and Labanotation in North America. In addition, several have been used for nondance purposes: Labanotation in industrial time-and-motion study, Benesh and Labanotation to record movement clinically (Benesh and McGuiness, 1974; Ryman, Patla and Calvert, 1984) and Eshkol-Wachmann to record behavioral patterns in animals (Golani, 1976). For input to a computer-based system, it is widely recognized as more general and analytic and thus more suitable than the Benesh system, although Benesh notation is particularly suited to the stylized movements of the ballet. Eshkol-Wachmann notation, while also analytic and general, is less useful since it has been less widely adopted. Labanotation, described extensively in the literature (e.g., Hutchinson, 1960), is the basis of the current system.

An example of Labanotation is shown in Figure 2.1. The score is written on a vertical staff where the central columns represent the support (normally, the left and right feet). Moving out from the center, successive columns represent the gestural movements of the left and right legs, the body, arms, and hands, The head is arbitrarily placed on the right. Symbols in appropriate columns of the staff indicate the level and direction of the movement of a body segment, while the time duration is indicated by the vertical length of the symbol. The great majority of Labanotation commands represent a simple instruction to move a limb segment (foot, upper arm, etc.) from its current orientation in space to a new orientation; the time for the start of the movement and its duration are specified. Thus the elemental movements are analogous to the phonemes of speech, where specific movements of the vocal tract produce a specified sound. Some Laban commands involve a shorthand which requires intelligent interpretation by a dancer (e.g., a jump). While specifying the velocity and acceleration associated with Laban movements (e.g., the speed and power or quality of the movement) is theoretically possible, doing so requires breaking the movement down into smaller and smaller parts, a prohibitiively tedious practice. In most cases, Labanotation leaves the dancer to interpret the quality of the movement rather freely. To provide this information Laban developed a parallel notation system, Effort-Shape.

Computer Interpretation of Notation

As noted above, the usefulness of all movement notation systems is diminished by their inherent complexity and difficulty of learning. As a consequence, a number of independent efforts have been made to implement computer systems to interpret notation. As an aid in the composition and editing of the movement notation score (Weber et al., 1978; Ryman et al., 1983) and as an interpreter which can animate a score and thus assist in learning (Calvert et al., 1978; Badler et al., 1979; Smoliar et al., 1977), the digital computer has been utilized in various ways. A computer-based editor for Benesh Notation is under development at the University of Waterloo (Ryman, Beatty, Booth and Singh, 1983) and a similar editor for Labanotation scores was developed by a group at the University of Pennsylvania (Smoliar and Weber, 1977). A rather different approach has been taken in Australia, where a computer-based Benesh Movement Language was developed at the University of Sydney (Herbison-Evans, 1979).

As one of the most general notation systems, Labanotation has been adopted by at least three computer-based schemes: Weber, Smoliar and Badler (1978) at the University of Pennsylvania, Savage and Officer (1977) at the University of Waterloo, and our own system at Simon Fraser University (Calvert et al., 1978, 1980, 1982).

Although it is possible to enter Labanotation symbols directly into a graphics terminal, this last effort has found it convenient to utilize an alphanumeric code instead of symbolic notation. The computer interpretation system analyzes the Labanotation commands and

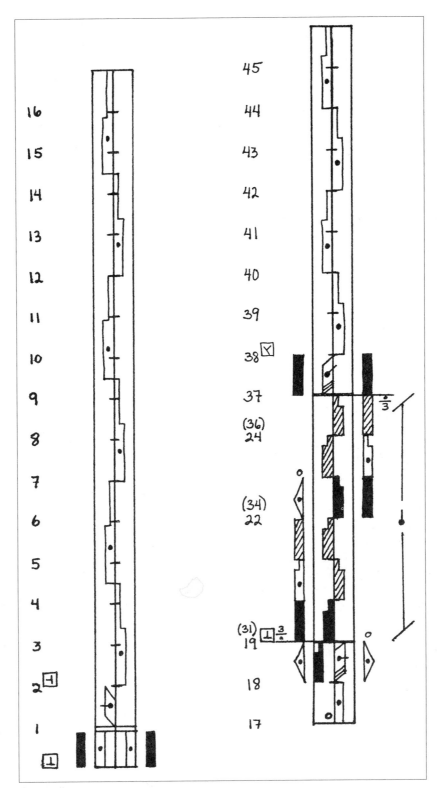

Figure 2.1
A simple Labanotation score.

translates them into a list of angles which each body segment must achieve in space. This data is in turn translated into the three-dimensional coordinates of each joint at each instant of time. The user selects the angle and distance from which the scene will be viewed and chooses an appropriate frame rate for the display. The interpreter for Labanotation is written in PASCAL and implemented on a VAX II 750-based IRIS Graphics Terminal. This high-quality raster graphics system generates either stick or simple fleshed-out figures with a screen resolution of 1204 x 768. The transportable interpretation system can also run on a variety of large and small computers including an Apple II microcomputer. Display interfaces have also been developed for a number of systems, but the smaller microcomputer systems run more slowly and provide lower-quality raster graphics. (Examples of output are shown in Figures 2.2 and 2.3). The simplest and fastest representation for the human body is a stick figure; a view of an isolated figure against a textured floor is shown in Figure 2.2. While such a figure gives all of the available information about the body movements, many observers find it somewhat unnatural, and so a fleshed-out display is also available; the version illustated in Figure 2.3 uses the technique developed by Badler et al. (1979) for simple raster graphics display. A better quality full-color figure produced on a digitized background on an IIS 512 x 512 display is illustrated in Figure 2.4.

The Use of Macros to Simplify a Score

Notation allows an observer to record the analysis of any movement pattern. Even with computer assistance, however, this operation can become tedious and repetitive in its detail.

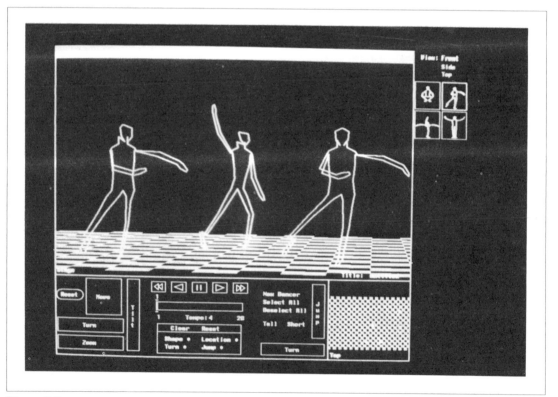

Figure 2.2
Line drawings of three figures on the IRIS Graphics Workstation.

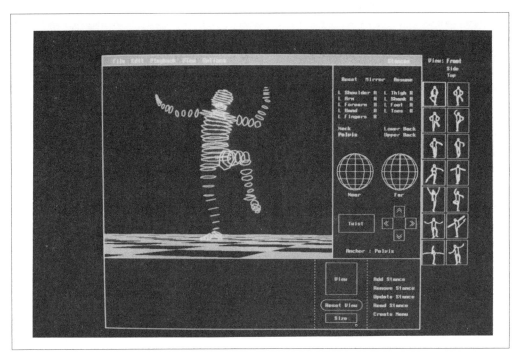

Figure 2.3
A more realistic figure generated with multiple contours.

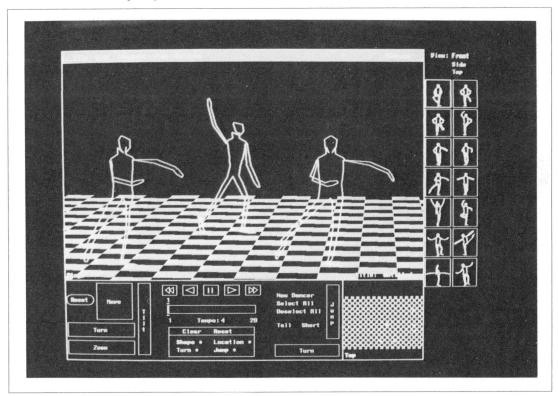

Figure 2.4
Line drawing of 3 figures on the IRIS Graphics Workstation.

In analogy to computer languages, we liken the notation to machine or assembly level code. Following this analogy, we have developed a set of powerful macros to aid the notator. In their simplest form, macro commands are programmed and named sequences of instructions. Specified parameters to modify the sequence in some simple way can enhance their usefulness considerably. The instruction sequence is not modified but important features, such as direction or speed, can be parameters of a macro. In more complicated ones, parameters result in conditional assembly of instructions, i.e., depending on some condition, the resulting sequence may be quite different. For example, WALK macro might have the following call:

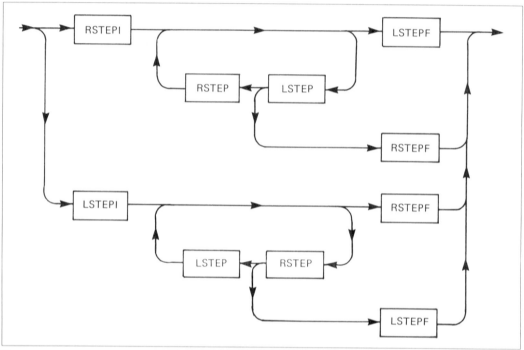

Figure 2.5
A Wirth diagram for a WALK Macro. The components are the initial left or right steps (LSTEP1 or RSTEP1), the continuing left or right steps (LSTEP or RSTEP) and the left and right final steps (LSTEPF or RSTEPF).

WALK { Distance; Steps; Stepsize; Direction; Startfoot; Style}

All the parameters, except the first, can have natural defaults. This WALK macro is, in fact, made up of a number of submacros and the beginnings of a syntax are seen in Figure 2.5, which shows a Wirth diagram for the WALK (Jensen and Wirth, 1975). The diagram shows that WALK involves an initial step (either right or left), followed by an arbitrary number of continuing steps on alternate legs terminated by a final step on the appropriate leg. Currently we have a library of several macros, including most of the standard ballet positions.

It should be clear that macros can conveniently prestore any sequence of Labanotation commands which may be used more than once. Simple parameters allow the sequence to be conditionally assembled for different numbers of repetitions, direction, and style, for example. Such macros can substantially shorten the notation of a movement sequence, In fact, this represents an intermediate step between the base notation and a more natural higher-level language.

A Movement Language in Film-making.

In planning the production of a film, the artistic director, working with the director and the scriptwriter, develops a series of storyboard sketches. These sketches provide the artist's visualization of the important elements of each scene. Preview systems, sometimes known as electronic storyboards, are being used by Robert Abel, Digital Productions and others to give relatively crude animation of a scene while it is being planned. Typically the equipment consists of a vector graphics display and a host computer. The objects present in a scene are entered in sufficient detail to produce line drawings which can be manipulated relative to each other in three dimensions. A director may set up keyframes manually by using knobs, a joystick, a mouse, or a tablet. Simple animation then gives a real-time display of the movement from keyframe to keyframe. When the director is satisfied with the compostion of the keyframes and the movement patterns between them, the coordinates and orientation of the objects and the orientation and movement of the cameras can be read out for shooting live action or can be fed directly into a database for production of computer animation.

Preview systems of this type greatly increase the opportunities for a director to experiment with a scene and play it many times before deciding how it will be shot. There are also great economic savings when shots and setups can be planned in detail to cut down shooting by as much as 50 per cent. Abel has estimated that a full-length feature film could be previewed for a cost approximately equal to that of one day's live action (*American Cinematographer*, 1982). However, because human animation is complex and difficult to specify, the systems developed so far have treated the human body as a single solid object. Obviously, this limits the preview system's usefulness for the director.

The application of a language for human movement to the production of animated films is obvious. Even for cartoons, however, most movements are still specified manually. To date, computer animation for feature films has been limited to what are essentially special effects and there have been only very simple attempts at human animation. Realistic animation requires the production of natural movement patterns for any object or character being simulated. While several existing systems have shown some capability in this area, particularly for nonarticulated objects, none are truly comprehensive and none provide for human animation. The work of Korein and Badler (1982), Zeltzer (1982a, b), and ourselves (Calvert et al., 1982) provides a starting point for human animation. Our commercial organization has experimented with our Labanotation-based system, but even with macros the scores become very long and cumbersome. Although the use of computers to produce totally realistic animation of human actors is not yet possible (animating a close-up of the face is particularly difficult), it is probably quite feasible to animate background characters in crowd scenes, etc.

Computer animation is being used fairly extensively in the production of advertisements for television and at least two major organizations, Lucasfilms and Digital Productions, are developing techniques to produce feature films (Demos et al., 1984); several films with significant sequences of computer animation have already been completed (e.g., "Tron" and "The Last Starfighter").

A Movement Language for Theater?

While to our knowledge, there has been no formal attempt in theater to use a preview system such as the electronic storyboard, the potential for such a system is obvious. The dynamics of

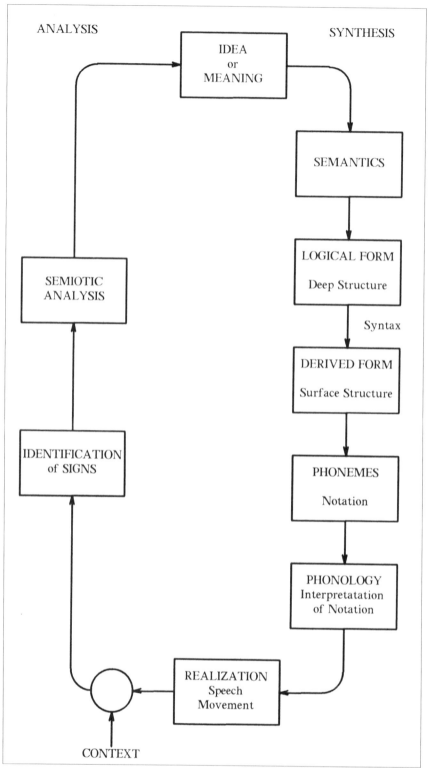

Figure 2.6
Analysis and synthesis in representing ideas with language.

production, however, are very different from film. While a film director can profitably use a simple animation system for solid objects, the theater director will definitely need a way to specify human movement. Also, the technical director may be interested in coupling a computerized script to such elements as the control of lighting.

Summary of Needs

The review indicates that there is a need for a flexible and natural method to specify and/or animate human movement for dance, film, and theater; such a system would presumably also find application in such fields as ergonomics. The current approaches, though, are rather primitive. Movement notation systems, typically elemental, detailed, and lacking in structure, are no substitute for a comprehensive language for movement. All indications point toward a more conceptual and fundamental approach to the representation and specification of movement.

A Theoretical Basis for a Language for Movement

Synthesis—Analogy to the Realization of Ideas as Speech

The theoretical approach which is followed here depends on a simple model for the role of a language. As illustrated in Figure 2.6, the essence of this model is that an idea to be communicated is first represented through a language (e.g., a natural language such as English) and then communicated through some physical realization (such as speech). This process involves synthesis. The inverse process takes place when an observer analyzes the physical realization and then represents it through language. From the representation in language the meaning is deduced. The analogy with speech, to be developed in more detail, is illustrated in Figure 2.7.

The originator of an idea, whether it is simple communication or a more complex narrative such as a play, a film, or the choreography of a dance, first represents this idea or set of ideas as a written script, possibly supplemented with graphics like those used for a movie storyboard. Whatever the medium, an appropriate vocabulary must be available. When ideas are represented in a natural language, the author's mastery of the language's grammar and knowledge of the semantics will guide the translation of the ideas into a particular logical form or deep structure (Chomsky, 1965). From this deep structure, the author's own style determines the derived form or surface structure. These are related by the rules of syntax.

If the communication is to be realized in the form of speech the reader's knowledge of phonology translates the text into a string of phonemes which are then produced as sounds by appropriate movement patterns controlling the muscles of the larynx, abdomen, and the mouth. The reader uses a knowledge of a rather complex set of rules to choose appropriate phonemes and appropriate intonation to represent the text. Computer synthesis of speech can be very good indeed when it is phoneme-driven (i.e., when a human selects the phonemes to represent the text) but is less successful when the computer program must implement the rules to determine the choice of phonemes and intonation.

Synthesis—The Realization of Ideas of Movement

There is a fairly clear analogy between the realization of an idea as speech and its realization as gestural communication or body language (Birdwhistell, 1970). Realization as a dance is often dominated by aesthetic considerations but otherwise is parallel to realizing the

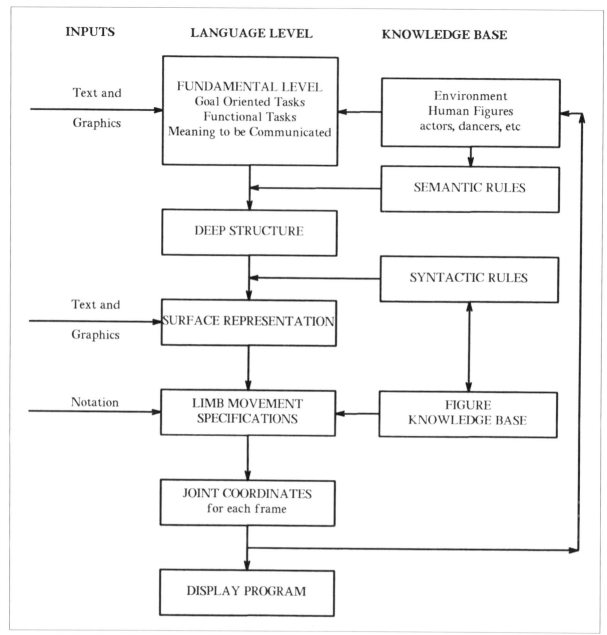

Figure 2.7
The role of language in realizing speech or movement.

narrative in a theater play or a film. However, although the overall process has similar features the steps involved in translating ideas into movement patterns are less clear. Discussion of representing meaning in a deep structure for dance (Williams, 1976) has produced no clear agreement on what is involved (Zelinger, 1979). Apart from some very preliminary discussion (Calvert et al., 1980), there has been no attempt to find a syntax for a movement language and there is no complete language for movement. In contrast to the relationship between text and speech, however, a number of notation schemes have been developed to represent elemental movements. These are most directly equivalent to a notation for specifying phonemes rather than to a natural language. Thus notation is rather explicit and fairly straightforward to interpret, by either a human or a computer. The principle difficulty with notation schemes is that they are necessarily elemental and extremely detailed; as a consequence they are difficult to learn and tedious to use. It should be clear that notation at this level is no substitute for a comprehensive natural language.

A Natural Language for Movement

The obvious need is to develop a *natural language* for human movement. Since the power of a language derives from the advantage of the structure present in the ideas to be expressed and in the movement patterns which realize them, it is necessary to formalize the semantics and syntax of movement. There will, in fact, be a hierarchy of grammars once a number of different forces impose structure on human movement. At a fundamental level, anatomical, physiological and biomechanical constraints limit the range of possible movement patterns, besides determining which patterns are most natural and easiest to perform. These constraints establish the patterns of functional movement, such as ambulation, feeding, and grooming, which generally play only a minor role in communication but may have a more important one in aesthetic performance. At a higher level are patterns determined culturally: communicative gestures, for example, are generally specific to a particular culture. At the highest level are the aesthetic movement patterns of dance. Each level is highly structured and should be amenable to formal syntactic description, but to our knowledge this effort has never been seriously attempted.

It should be noted that the analogy to communication in general and to speech in particular is not complete. Some movements are purposeful but have no *meaning*; they are merely functional. For example an instruction to "walk across the street" or "drink from the cup" does not necessarily communicate meaning. Thus we must broaden the role of meaning to include goal-oriented and functional patterns.

Analysis—Semiotics

The processes described above all involve synthesis. Starting from the ideas of an author, choreographer, or other communicator, a formal or informal language description is derived and this in turn is translated by a speaker, an actor, a dancer, or a computer into a physical realization of the original idea. Some help in determining a formal language to describe movement patterns can be obtained from studying the inverse process of analysis. The syntax of a language is helpful in determining the meaning of text or speech but semiological analysis is still only a primitive tool for the analysis of the total meaning of a narrative text, a play, a film, or a dance performance (Berger, 1982). Semiological analysis (or semiotics) involves the identification of signs and relations and the deduction of meaning from them. Anyone interpreting a performance is using a personal set of rules to identify signs in it, although not always consciously aware of these rules. The signs play a role analogous to words or even phrases in text, and the rules for the relationships between them are analogous to the syntax of the text. While semiotics is still relatively primitive, work on developing a language for film, for example (Metz, 1974), is certainly very relevant to the development of a general language for movement. Some general ideas for a semiotics of dance have been discussed by Zelinger (1979).

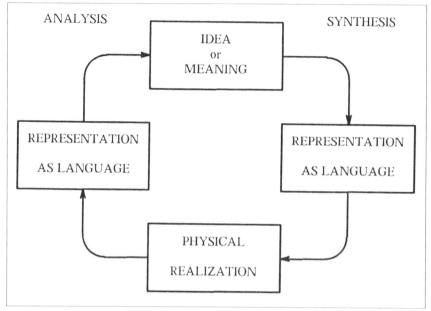

Figure 2.8
The functional components of the movement language.

Functional Design of the Movement Language

Ideally, the language of the system should be available to the user at three levels. These are illustrated in Figure 2.8 and will be discussed in turn in terms of their inputs, function, and knowledge base.

It should be emphasized that the normal input at all levels for this language will involve not only text, but also numerical data and graphics; the input will typically be entered interactively at a graphics workstation and will have text and graphic sketches side by side.

Fundamental Level

Specification at this level is in terms of the goal to be achieved, the function to be performed, or the meaning to be communicated. Thus typical inputs might include:

"Drink from the small glass on the table."

"Walk across the room and open the door."

"Stand up and walk toward Figure B, shake hands with Figure B."

"Ronde de jambe á terre en dehors with the right into 4th position devant—demi plié facing corner 1."

"The group sits on the floor. They talk. They extend their hands and clasp each other's arms. Then they try to stand. Becky has her back to everyone. All stand except Becky."

The common feature of all inputs at this level is that they are incomplete, to a greater or lesser degree of specificity; they describe a goal-oriented task, functional movement, or sequence of a dance, but in all cases substantial information is missing. Required for interpretation of these instructions and their translation into a complete and specific set of instructions are a knowledge base which includes information on all important aspects of the environment (dimensions of the room, stage or set; size and placement of the furniture and miscellaneous objects) as well as figures present (the term 'figure' will be used in lieu of 'actor,' 'dancer,' etc.). This level of input can be derived directly from a script or screenplay.

Deep Structure

Semantic rules are then used to translate the Fundamental Level input into something analogous to the Deep Structure of natural language. This transformation, using Semantic Rules, involves filling in all missing information regarding the general movement of all figures but still leaving low-level details unspecified. For example, the start time, end time and path of a walk would be fully specified but the number of steps and individual style (both of which depend on characteristics of the particular figure) would still be unspecified. An important feature of this transformation would be the use of sensible defaults for unspecified parameters where the value cannot be derived from the knowledge base. The Deep Structure, being an internal representation, is not planned to allow input at this level.

The Deep Structure will have a form similar to the Surface Representation but will differ inasmuch as many different Surface Representations can be derived from one Deep Structure. This variety is due to the different body dimensions, movement characteristics, and even mood of the different figures. These differences are resolved by reference to the figure knowledge base and the Syntactic Rules which apply to each figure.

Surface Representation

This level derives input from the Deep Structure but can also receive independent external input. One example of this input might take the following form:

"Figure A extends right elbow joint until lower arm and hand are horizontal. Arm extends, maintaining lower arm and hand horizontal, until open hand is at position x=31, y=65, z=96. Hand closes until thumb-to-finger clearance is equal to diameter of glass. Flex elbow and maintain hand horizontal until hand is 2.0 from mouth."

It can be seen that this input comprises a very specific set of instructions on how to pick up a glass and prepare to drink from it; it will be noted, however, that most limb angles are still unspecified. Generally this description will be much more detailed than that found in even a heavily annotated script or screenplay.

Limb movement specifications

From the Surface Representation, the lowest level of the language is derived by applying the Syntactic Rules for the figure in question. Thus the details of body size will be taken into account as well as anatomical and biomechanical limits on movement. A more difficult development will be a method to give preference to movements which are more natural and even to the habitual movement patterns and styles of individuals. The Limb Movement Specifications are represented by an extended version of Labanotation and enhanced by our macros. Thus it will be possible for the user to provide direct input at this level. Also possible will be the editing and fine-tuning notation derived from higher levels of the system, although it will not necessarily be possible to perform an inverse transformation to reflect these low-level changes in the high-level script. Direct input from live subjects equipped with goniometers and other instrumentation is also possible.

Implementation

The system outlined above is comprehensive and ambitious. Its full implementation will require many years of work devoted to developing the knowledge bases for the various expert systems required to capture the terminology of the director/writer/artist, the physical characteristics of the set/environment, the representation and shape of objects and human figures to be animated and the movement of these figures and objects. An attractive feature of this problem, however, is its potential to be developed hierarchically. Thus, a simple language system can be implemented very quickly indeed; most of the elements already exist. This simple system will have a simple user-machine interface and a miniscule knowledge base for the expert system.

Implementing the language system will make extensive use of some recent developments in hardware and software. Advances in inexpensive but powerful microprocessors and high-resolution bitmapped graphical displays have provided the basis for sophisticated workstations. A workstation provides a user interface with interactive graphics, a rich software environment, a very powerful (32-bit) standalone processor and high-bandwidth connection by local area network to other processors, file servers, etc.; workstations are ideal for the development of this language system. Research in artificial intelligence has defined the methodology for building expert systems and their associated knowledge bases; expert systems provide a consistent approach to the formalization of the syntactic and semantic rules of the proposed language. The following major phases of the implementation are planned:

Consolidation in a State-of-the-Art Hardware/Software Environment. This phase is essentially complete. A Sun Microsystems workstation provides the user interface and the software environment. The Sun, running Unix on a 68000 processor, is connected by Ethernet to two VAXs, other Suns and an IRIS graphics terminal. The high-resolution bitmapped display and the powerful windowing capability are ideal for the user interface, which requires the parallel input of scripts and graphic sketches. The animated output is produced on a Silicon Graphics IRIS 1200 terminal, which has a powerful capability for three-dimensional transformations and the real-time animation of line drawings and simple solid figures.

Development of the Language Expert System. Determining the appropriate vocabulary and the knowledge base will require extensive interaction with the directors and artists involved in filmmaking, animation, and theater. The expert system is being developed in C and C-Prolog on a Sun. The prototype, which is called "The Director's Apprentice," focuses on those aspects of the language which are particularly relevant to filmmaking.

Development of the Human Animation Expert System. This phase requires the buildup of the knowledge base for the physical parameters, the anatomical and physiological constraints, and the natural movement patterns of a human actor or actress. It is required to implement the surface structure. Already completed is preliminary work on a flexible system to build up animation sequences interactively on the IRIS terminal.

Development of Planner for Movement in a Cluttered World. This aspect draws heavily on parallel work in the planning of robotic movement in a cluttered environment. It is only one example of the autonomous problem-solving capability necessary to implement the Deep Structure inputs.

Conclusions

While the theoretical development presented in this chapter is rather general, initial implementation is expected to be specific to different areas of applications. This specificity not only makes the problem more manageable, but also facilitates the definition of the hard problems which must be addressed. It is interesting to note that as development of this language has moved from an abstract theoretical framework to a detailed design for practical implementation, our view of it has changed. It is now viewed as a multi-component system made up of a very sophisticated interface for user interaction, a set of hierarchically organized expert systems and knowledge bases, and a high-quality display for the output of animation. Perhaps this change should not be surprising, for these are just the components which the human organism has evolved for language communication.

References

American Cinematographer (1982, July). (Special Issue on Computer Assisted Filmaking).

Badler, R., and Smoliar, S.W. (1979). Digital representation of human movement. *Computing Surveys, 11,* 19–38.

Benesh, R., and Benesh, J. (1956). *An Introduction to Benesh Dance Notation.* London: A.C. Black.

Benesh, R., and McGuinness, J. (1974). Benesh movement, notation and medicine. *Physiotherapy, 60,* 176–178.

Berger, A. A. (1982). *Media Analysis Techniques.* Sage COMTEXT Series. Beverly Hills: Sage Publications, *10.*

Birdwhistell, R.L. (1970). *Kinetics and Context: Essays on Body Movement Communication.* Philadelphia, Pennsylvania: University of Pennsylvania Press.

Calvert, T. W. (1983). Computer assisted filmmaking. In *Proceedings of Graphics Interface 83 Conference.* Edmonton, Alberta.

Calvert, T. W., Chapman, J. & Patla, A. (1982). Aspects of the kinematic simulation of human movement. *IEEE Computer Graphics and Applications, 2,* 41–50.

Calvert, T. W., Chapman, J. & Patla, A. (1980). The integration of subjective and objective data in animation of human movement. *Computer Graphics, 14,* 198–203.

Calvert, T. W., Chapman, J. & Landis, J. (1979). Notation of Dance with computer assistance. In D. T. Taplin (Ed.), *New Directions in Dance.* Toronto, Canada: Pergamon Press, 169–178.

Calvert, T. W., Chapman, J. (1978). Notation of movement with computer assistance. *Proceedings of the ACM Annual Conference, 2,* 731–736.

Chomsky, N. (1965). *Aspects of the Theory of Syntax.* Cambridge: MIT Press.

Demos, G., Brown, M. & Weinberg, R. (1984). Digital scene simulation: The synergy of computer technology and human activity. *Proceedings of the IEEE, 72,* 22–31.

Eshkol, N. & Wachmann, A. (1958). *Movement Notation.* London: Weidenfield and Nicholson.

Golani, I. (1976). Homeostatic motor processes in mannalian interactions: A choreography of display. In P. P. G. Bateson and P. H. Klopfer, (Eds), *Perspectives in Ethology, 2,* (2nd chapter). New York: Plenum.

Herbison-Evans, D. A. (1979). A human movement language for computer animation. In J. Tobias (Ed.), *Language Design and Programming Methodology.* New York: Springer-Verlag.

Hutchinson, A. (1960). *Labanotation.* New York: Theater Art Books.

Jensen, K. & Wirth, N. (1975). *Pascal-User Manual and Report.* New York: Springer-Verlag.

Korein, J. U. & Badler, N. I. (1982). Techniques for generating the goal directed motion of articulated structures. *IEEE Computer Graphics and Applications, 2,* 71–81.

Metz, C. (1974). *Film Language.* New York: Oxford University Press.

Ryman, R., Beatty, J. C., Booth, K. S. & Singh, A. (1983). A computerized editor for Benesh movement notation. *CORD Dance Research Journal, 16* (1),

Ryman, R. J., Patna, A. & Calvert, T. (1983). Use of Labanotation for clinical analysis of movement. In *Proceedings of the International Congress Kinetography Laban.*

Savage, G. J. & Officer, J. (1987). Choreography: An interactive computer model for choreography. In *Proceedings of the 5th Man-Machine Communications Conference.* Calgary, Alberta.

Schelflen, A. E. (1974). *How Behavior Means.* Garden City: Anchor Books.

Smoliar, S. W. & Weber, L. (1977). Using the computer for a semantic representation of Labanotation. In S. Lusigman & J. S. North (Eds.), *Computing and the Humanities.* Waterloo, Ontario: University of Waterloo Press, 253–261.

Weber, L., Smoliar, S. W., & Badler, N. J. (1978). An architecture for the simulation of human movement. *Proceedings of the ACM Annual Conference, 2,* 737–745.

Williams, D. (1976). Deep structures of the dance. *Journal of Human Movement Studies, 2,* 123–144 & 155–181.

Zellinger, J. (1979). Semiotics and theatre dance. In D. T. Taplin (Ed.), *New Directions in Dance.* Toronto: Pergamon Press.

Zeltzer, D. (1982). Representation of complex animated figures. *Proceedings of Graphics Interface.* Toronto, 205–212.

Zeltzer, D. (1982). Motor control techinques for figure animation. *IEEE Computer Graphics and Applications, 2,* 53–59.

3 A Computational Alternative to Effort Notation*

Norman I. Badler
Department of Computer and Information Science
University of Pennsylvania, Philadelphia

A significant portion of our activities and perceptions are associated with the performance, observation, description, or recording of human movement. It is a challenge to the current state of knowledge in computer science to similarly represent, simulate, and integrate these differing manifestations of human movement since they touch on such seemingly diverse areas as computer graphics, computer vision, robotics, and computational linguistics (Badler, et al., 1980). In this exposition we shall discuss the philosophy and methodology behind our research into the computational understanding of human movement, concentrating on the issues of movement representation, movement synthesis, and task specification. While our primary emphasis will be on performance, that is, the animation or simulation of natural human motion, we cannot avoid inquiring what our representational decisions would imply for a general theory of human movement understanding.

We will try to examine human movement in the most global view possible, namely, that a movement representation should be at least sympathetic to the needs and character of each modality: performance (or control), observation, language description, or symbolic recording. Our own research, and certainly that of others, has touched all these areas: for example, computer graphics for human motion synthesis (Badler & Badler, 1978; Calvert et al., 1980; Zeltzer, 1986; Korein & Badler, 1983; Magenat-Thalmann & Thalman, 1985; Lineman, 1985; Emmett, 1985), computer vision for motion and shape analysis (O'Rourke & Badler, 1980; Akita, 1982; Lee & Chen, 1985), movement notations for symbolic motion representation (Ginsberg & Maxwell, 1986; Weber et al., 1978; Badler & Smoliar, 1979; Calvert et al., 1982), language for motion verb characterization (Miller, 1972; Badler, 1978; Gangel, 1985), and robotics for path planning and goal-directed behavior (Korein & Badler, 1982; Korein, 1985). Having originally examined motion descriptions based on vision-based input data (Badler, 1975), the inadequacy of this view by itself is keenly felt. Such descriptions may serve as a target for information reduction, but are apt to be the product of convenience dictated by the observational task at hand. Such a description differentiates between phenomena of interest, possibly incorporating rudimentary notions of direction, velocity, and shape. Likewise, representations derived solely from language (Schank, 1975) omit essential information needed to reconstruct an acceptable performance.

---

*©Norman I. Badler, University of Pennsylvania.

By turning to representations derived from graphical performance or physical object control (for example, robotics), we get a different perspective. In particular, a graphical or physical performance will verify that a representation is adequate to characterize some (hopefully broad) class of human movement. It is this adequacy that permits experimentation based on empirical data (say from observed movements) and parametric variation to control or tune the result.

The role of natural language descriptions is to expose the salient features of human motion interpreted (by a culture) as significant events. In particular, we find language has evolved rich verb and adverbial vocabularies to permit the description and expression of subtle movements. In fact language goes even further by imputing behavior, emotion, and intent to movement, even when that motion is not obviously attributable to human-appearing agents (Michotte, 1946). While such information is available subconsciously via our cognitive systems, it may also be instantiated in language (or physically acted out, for that matter). Therefore we assume the existence of a transformation which maps some of these subconscious perceptions into tangible (and essential) components of a motion representation. It appears that some of this information can be captured; how much is not clear, though we will propose a model here.

Finally, we use movement notations as a source of symbolic representations derived from empirical observation and analysis over many years by many observers of numerous subjects. The impact of such systems is that they provide one of the only possible bases for establishing completeness: that is, does the representation cover, in its variations, the known scope and range of human movement? Language also provides some of this scope, but does not lend itself so readily to analysis.

We proceed by examining some of the representational issues which arise in considering the influence of these requirements.

Representation Requirements

Movements of human or robot agents may be characterized at many different levels. A purely geometric level of description as changing coordinates, though necessary, is insufficient as a comprehensive basis for understanding motion. A simple gesture such as closing the hand may be described by joint angles, by paths of the fingertips, by flexion of muscles, by the concept "grasp," or by the intention "shake hands." Each type of description is useful in different contexts, and a natural hierarchy of levels seems to appear. To discuss a movement representation therefore is to establish what descriptive levels are important and what attributes or characteristics are adequate to completely "cover" the space of possible movements at each level. We will return to this issue later, after establishing a plausible representation scheme in which to formulate higher level motion or action descriptions (Fishwick, 1986).

Viewing movement hierarchically focuses attention on descriptive or conceptual levels, that is, the refinement or generalization of a movement at a different level of detail. Performance of a particular motion, however, requires the interaction or combination of effects from many sources. While geometric object descriptions lend themselves to a hierarchic view (Clark, 1976; Badler & Bajcsy, 1978; Marr & Nishihara, 1981), motions are dictated by simultaneous interacting influences. Muscle tension, external forces, joint limits, path constraints, expressive purpose, intention, and the context of temporally adjacent activities all affect human movement. A more general approach to movement understanding therefore would cover at least the following aspects of a motion:

- *The geometry, kinematics, and dynamics of the agent*
  The individual differences in people and their anthropometry must be taken into account. Motion is significantly affected by the kinematics of jointed objects, such as joint limits, reachable points, and comfort zones. Dynamics describes the force or effort influencing motion, whether actual or perceived, and may be independent of motion path. Dynamics also involves the inherent strength of the agent to initiate or resist motion.

- *Any goal-directed or intentional acts of which the movement was part*
  Much human motion is intentional, even if unconscious: the achievement of reach goals, negotiation through a space, maintenance of balance, and comfortable distribution of weight.

- *The agent's attitude toward the environment, and its general mode of behavior*
  The interpretation of any particular motion is highly dependent on the environmental and personal context; thus a "threatening" gesture in a social context may be merely "defensive" in an athletic one. Motions which are part of an ongoing task or activity may be perceived as more global entities rather than isolated movements.

- *What, if anything, is signified*
  For example, sign language research shows that certain seeming variations in a movement are understood as the same sign, while others are not. Often movements along the same spatial path and toward the same spatial goal may signify very different intents, such as "touch," "press," and "punch."

- *Any synchronization or concurrency relations the movement depends on or is derived from*
  Motions may occur in isolation, in sequence, in parallel, or in any overlapped or superimposed combination. Some of these relationships were studied in the motion context (Badler et al., 1980), in language (Allen, 1984; Waltz, 1982), and in task-level reasoning (Vere, 1983; Fishwick, 1986). They may also overlap, mask, dominate, accentuate, or modify one another, as has been demonstrated with facial motions (Platt & Badler, 1981; Platt, 1985). The movements may occur compressed or extended in time, or be subject to environmental constraints or control requirements. For example, the actions of a group of athletes on a team is subject to the rules of the game as much as the particular instantaneous circumstances of the play.

Of course, these factors are not orthogonal to one another, but interact and interrelate in complex ways. Part of our task is therefore to organize motion information so that we can hope to control motion to the extent that the different factors can be investigated at appropriate levels.

The central "core" of the movement understanding methodology is a movement representation and its interpretation by computer simulation. The reason we insist upon interpretation will be clarified further in the next section. In succeeding sections we will examine particular aspects of the motion representation and show how each component is essential to effective motion synthesis and how its semantics might be implemented.

Requirements for Representation Primitives

In keeping with the general concerns expressed above, we enunciate several criteria deemed essential to the design of an effective motion representation. To focus the effort, we will define a movement representation as a system in which *any movement may be decomposed into "primitives" with implementable semantics.* We require these primitives to meet certain constraints:

- *Descriptive significance*
  Abstractions of position, motion, and dynamics must allow comparison between motions independent of the source of the description. It should not matter, for example, whether motions have been obtained through direct sensor measurements, mathematical functions, or human interactive design.

  This issue implies that mere visual images are not sufficient for a motion representation; even an extensive "film library" is not in the form of primitives that may be readily used as the basis for simulating arbitrary motion patterns. There is no index upon which similarity or differences between two motions may be easily judged. There may not even be agreement between observers as to the name or type of motion being performed. The fact that most imagery is two-dimensional is an additional complication, but if the images were from multiple viewpoints or even holographic, the objection would still stand.

  A similar objection can be raised to descriptions consisting of natural language text. Though there may be cultural agreement on the meaning of an utterance, the actual process of converting the description to action may be subject to widely varying interpretations, for example, via "acting."

- *Modifiability through generally accessible methods*
  This issue implies that a motion representation must permit the symbolic or computational modification of a motion primitive in order to create a wide class of related or similar motions. "Generally accessible" implies eliminating choices such as libraries of artist-drawn animations, since the creation of natural-appearing hand-drawn animations is not a widespread skill. At the minimum, this constraint argues for parametric descriptions, though we need not commit to a specific set of parameters yet.

- *Independence of specific individuals*
  This issue again rejects the film or artist-drawn library approach, and also disallows more detailed but still joint- or segment-specific motion data collected from an individual. Thus while such motion may be used as the basis of a specific animation (Calvert et al., 1980; Ginsberg et al., 1986; Emmett, 1985), it is not obvious how such a motion would change if it were applied to another individual with different body dimensions, weight, strength, posture, etc.

- *Independence of specific motion characteristics*
  This issue emphasizes the need for a parametric approach, though now the problem is the motions within an individual and the possible ways they can be combined, compounded, executed in parallel or sequence, or inhibit or permit other motions, etc. Thus the primitives must describe possible actions of body components and be subject to synchronization and modification by other primitives. In addition, we expect physical factors to be separable: for example, the path of a motion should be separable from the kinetics of motion along the path. Again, representations of the library type cannot deal effectively with the computational explosion of possibilities inherent in arbitrary human motion.

In constructing a movement representation we have been very concerned with its capabilities to describe sufficient information for a "performance" by computer synthesized graphic images (Badler & Smoliar, 1979). This point of view has been very fruitful in deciding what characteristics of a movement description and hence of an adequate representation, are necessary. The important concept is that movement synthesis considerations demand consistent implementable semantics. If a computer system could produce any movement specified by the appropriate descriptive parameters, then it would also verify that a representation was an adequate knowledge base with which to describe or notate observed movement. Thus, for example, if the representation cannot express the differences between "press" and "punch," it would not have sufficient means to distinguish these actions if actually observed.

Labanotation

Symbolic representations of many movement properties are found in Labanotation (Hollerbach, 1980), a movement notation system originated over 50 years ago by Rudolf Laban. Though several notation systems exist, few come close to meeting the criteria for a movement representation. We initially studied Labonatation (Badler & Smoliar, 1979), basing the choice on several factors deemed essential for effective motion specification:

• its redundant means of expressing a movement

• its methods for handling sequence, concurrency, and phrasing

• its capabilities for arbitrary frames of reference

• its incorporation of goal-directed actions

• its essentially 'digital' symbol system.

We abstracted these Labanotation properties into a set of five "primitive movement concepts" (Weber et al., 1978) (directions, revolutions, facings, shapes, and contacts) concerned only with the location and relations of body joints or surfaces in space. Significantly, these primitives do not cover dynamic effects (force, acceleration, torque, etc.), muscular movements (bulges, contractions, etc.) or facial expressions (Calvert et al., 1980; Parke, 1982). Thus a motion specification in this system actually describes the final goal and some constraints on the path rather than the internal method by which it is achieved (Calvert et al., 1980). Directions generally describe positions to be achieved by body parts, or directions in which the entire body is to move. Revolutions include rotations and twists by given angles. Facings are goal-directed rotations which require a body surface to achieve a desired orientation. A shape is either a path along which a body or body part moves, or a spatial shape (position or configuration) which some subset of the body is to achieve. Contacts are generally relationships such as touches, supports, contains, etc., between two or more bodies, body parts, or environmental points. All the primitives share notions of duration, fixed end, and reference coordinate system.

Updating the Labanotation Model

We have recently come to view movement somewhat differently. The evolution of this early motion representation is motivated not only by current efforts in three-dimensional computer animation (Linehan, 1985; Magnenat-Thalman & Thalman, 1985), but also by practice in robotics (Paul, 1972; Lozano-Perez & Wesley, 1979; Hollerbach, 1980; Paul, 1981; Derby, 1983) and motion analysis (O'Rourke & Badler, 1980; Tsotsos et al., 1980). We distinguish four different kinds of movement primitives:

• *Changes:* rotations by a given angle or translation along a given path or direction

- *Goals:* achievement of a given location and/or orientation for a body point (Korein & Badler, 1982)

- *Paths:* curves in space along which points may move

- *Dynamics:* kinetics or forces which control or affect a motion.

The former "primitive movement concepts" are easily subsumed into the first three of these four primitives. The new primitive, *dynamics*, will be discussed in the next section. A comparison of the categories of the "old" representation (Badler & Smoliar, 1979; Weber et al., 1978) with respect to this new representation appears in Table 3.1.

In Table 3.1, a *reach* refers to the kinematic achievement of a location in space by some body point and an orientation to the kinematic achievement of an *orientation* of a body point. The

Table 3.1: Comparison of "old" and "new" movement representations.	
"old"	"new"
DIRECTION (movement)	Change in position
DIRECTION (position)	Reach goal
REVOLUTION (rotate)	Change in orientation
REVOLUTION (twist)	Change in orientation
FACING	Orientation goal
SHAPE (movement)	Sequence of reach goals or "key-parameter" locations
SHAPE (position)	"Key-parameter" positions
CONTACT	Sequence or set of reach and orientation goals

"key-parameter" concept refers to a set of parametric values for particular manipulable variables of the body such as point angles, reach position, body location, etc.

Changes, goals, and paths must have associated with them durations, starting times, and reference coordinate systems. We can assume that the original specification is adequate in that regard (Weber et al., 1978). Items such as fixed ends of a reach goal are indicated by zero changes in that body point in an appropriate coordinate reference frame (Badler et al., 1978; Girard & Maciejewski, 1985). Thus the shoulder might be the fixed end for an arm reach to position and orient a hand with respect to some object. The former contact primitive is subsumed into time-marked sets of one or more goals achieved sequentially and in parallel as needed. The semantics of determining those goals is left to a higher level process (Badler et al., 1983; Zeltzer, 1986; Gangel, 1985; Fishwick, 1986).

Concurrency

The task of synchronizing concurrent actions and handling multiple constraints is passed to a control system rather than being explicitly embedded in the representation. A parallel control algorithm had been advocated earlier for this purpose (Badler & Smoliar, 1979). The essential features of this control were:

- joint "processors" which interpreted parallel streams of motion primitive "instructions" as programs

- a special processor to handle movements of the center of gravity, and

- a global monitor to synchronize local changes to a global, constrained body model and thus process concurrent overlapping motion primitives.

We can relax the control model by viewing the body parametrically, that is, any specified point on the body may be controlled by specifying a sequence of one or more values over time for it. Paths are themselves a sequence of parameter values. The parameter values may be affected by more than one primitive, for example, the position of the body's center of gravity may be affected by the path of movement, inertia, and external forces (Badler & Smoliar, 1979; Girard & Maciejewski, 1985). It is the responsibility of the animator and the simulation semantics to resolve any discrepancies. The particular interactions of the dynamics primitives are new and will be examined carefully in the next section.

Kinetics and Dynamics

A key feature of human movement virtually ignored in earlier representation efforts is its kinetic or dynamic quality: the manner in which the body moves in terms of force, effort, exertion, energy, etc. Strictly speaking, *kinetic* refers to motion described by position, velocity, and acceleration, while *dynamics* means motion induced by forces. Until recently, the term dynamics has been applied to both situations in the motion control and representation literature. We will separate the cases when concerned with the method of control; otherwise we will use the broader meaning when there should be no confusion.

Kinetics and dynamics may be more significant, in an expressive or intentional sense, than the actual path. For example, variations in kinetics can alter the message conveyed in American Sign Language (Klima & Bellugi, 1979; Loomis et al., 1983). Kinetics and dynamics information appear only implicitly in the representations derived from the study of movement notation systems because:

- Labanotation (or for that matter, nearly any other notation) does not convey dynamic information other than timing (duration) which gives approximate velocity and perhaps accent which yields a very qualitative force.

- Motion semantics have been mostly concerned with visually smooth implementation of each primitive motion, not of the details of that motion during its execution nor with its continuity in the context of temporally adjacent motions, and

- The computational models must include capabilities for understanding some minimal physics associated with body mass, force, inertia, gravity, balance, etc. (Badler et al., 1980).

Computer animation done without concern for motion dynamics looks flat or mechanical at best; discontinuous or jerky at worst.

Previous efforts at incorporating kinetics and dynamics into computer generated animation have focused on explicit velocity or acceleration functions (Mezei & Zivian, 1971; Catmull, 1972; Herbison-Evans, 1978), artist-drawn keyframes (Burtnyk & Wein, 1976; Platt, 1985), smooth spline functions (Shelley & Greenberg, 1982; Sturman, 1984; Kochanek & Bartels,

1984; Steketee & Badler, 1985), or actual data from human subjects (Calvert et al., 1980; Baecker, 1969; Zeltzer, 1982; Ginsberg & Maxwell, 1986). Recently, dynamics have been used to control human or articulated figures (Armstrong et al., 1987; Wilhelms, 1987; Girard, 1987). Our own examination of the motion control problem has focused on alternative notation systems combined with physical and graphical motion models suited to the complexity of the human figure.

In searching for a representational basis for the dynamic qualities of movement, we examined a notation system complementary to Labanotation called Effort-Shape notation (Dell, 1970; Bartenieff, 1980). Unfortunately, the semantics of this system are not defined quantitatively, so we have interpreted it freely to produce something more amenable to computation. We believe this to be a reasonable approach since our intent is not to "computerize" Effort-Shape, or another notational system as we and others have attempted to do. Rather, we use these systems to aid in comprehending the scope and variety of human movement so that our representations are more likely to cover the space of possibilities. In the remainder of this paper we describe the influence of kinetics and dynamics considerations on a motion representation and sketch possible implementations of its semantics.

Effort-Shape Notation

Effort-Shape Notation is a system for describing the qualities of movement rather than its positional result or the actual method of achievement. Of the two major components of the notation, "Shape" (the way the body shapes itself in space, for example, rising, widening, advancing, etc.) is less important to the present discussion and appears to be partially derivable from the positional and directional information already present in the representational components shown in Table 3.1. The Effort component, however, provides some interesting insights into new properties required for an effective and complete motion representation.

The Effort dimension (Fig. 3.1) consists of four factors: flow, weight, time, and space. Flow describes the changes in the quality of muscle tension in the body as it varies between free and bound; weight, changes in body or limb weight between light or strong; time, changes in the quality of a movement between sustained and sudden; and space, changes in the spatial focus between direct and indirect. By examining what motion characteristics are expressed by these factors, we may attempt to quantify essential semantics.

We approach the incorporation of kinetics and dynamics into a motion representation by analyzing the Effort factors along four computationally feasible paths. The first modulates control and randomness in motion, the second involves representing physical characteristics of a specific joint and its "constellation" of muscles, the third models gross acceleration and velocity parameters, and the fourth phrases sequences of movements.

Joint changes, goals, and randomness
Executing a movement may depend on knowing whether a particular goal point is intended. The space Effort factor allows the expression of direct or indirect actions. Only the former can be interpreted as a positional goal in space; a positional goal is inappropriate for the latter. A reasonable interpretation is that indirect movements are described by changes in joint angles rather than by goal positions. A movement described solely by joint rotations (changes) is apt to have a weak sense of focus or directionality at the end of the moving limb. One way, therefore, to obtain less direct movements is to express them by joint rotations only.

FLOW

Free		Bound
easy flowing		controlling the flow
streaming out		streaming inward
abandoned		holding back, restrained
ready to go		ready to stop

SPACE

Direct		Indirect
zeroing in		encompassing focus
pinpointing		flexible

WEIGHT

Stong		Light
impactful		using fine touch
vigorous		airy
powerful		delicate

TIME

Sudden		Sustained
urgent		taking time
hasty		leisurely

Figure 3.1
The EFFORT qualities

The point we must make here is that indirectness is a quality which may be desirable in certain human movements, and we should seek to permit and control its presence, not avoid it in the representation. It is perhaps not surprising that people have difficulty reaching specific goals or positioning other mechanisms such as robots when restricted solely to motion changes by specific joint angles. Robotics, for example, relies on Cartesian or rectilinear control of end effector position (goal) over numerical specification of joint angles (Paul, 1979). The joint angles are computed by inverse kinematics. Position control through teleoperators or direct manipulation of the three-dimensional body or linkage can overcome this limitation, but this option is not normally available to the graphical animator. Some of the problems with this approach are the lack of suitable sensors to digitize the actual human body positions and the necessity to control and generalize the motions thus input (Calvert et al., 1982; Ginsberg & Maxwell, 1986). We would expect that the class of motions best input by such direct sensing techniques should be the indirect ones; indeed this is supported by the extreme difficulty in using joint angle positions alone to achieve convincing goal directed motions such as walking. One further problem is encountered if joint angle changes to a human figure model are implemented carelessly: the relative changes introduce a small but measurable amount of numerical error into the joint position. The problem and its numerical analysis solution in a human animation environment have been neatly documented by Herbison-Evans and Richardson (Herbison-Evans & Richardson, 1981).

Another mechanism for achieving indirectness is by stochastic motion processes: large-scale Brownian or fractal motions (Mandelbrot, 1977) of body joints. Similar stochastic motion processes have been used for fire, fireworks, and grass special effects (Reeves, 1983; Reeves, 1985). While we have not yet attempted to create such fractal (and hopefully indirect Effort) motions, incorporating a suitable random number generator and its parameters into the existing motion control structure is not difficult.

Random perturbations added to joint angles are unlikely to produce more directed motions, but added to Cartesian goals will increase indirectness. Thus we propose a continuum from direct to indirect which is represented as a linear combination of joint angles derived from explicit Cartesian goals and joint angle changes. "Pure" direct combination of joint angles are derived from explicit Cartesian goals and joint angle changes. "Pure" direct motions require no additional joint angle change specifications; "pure" changes require no goals. In between are a range of potential motions biased by some additional joint angle adjustment. An example of such a combination might be a forward reach goal for an arm biased by an explicit shoulder and elbow flexions. The kinematic position computed on the basis of the reach would be modified by the elbow and shoulder changes. The hand might achieve the general goal direction but fail to achieve it precisely, perhaps by falling short and low of the mark.

Unfortunately, it appears that small amounts of disorder do not give rise to exactly the kind of "natural" gestural and postural effects we would expect (Struman, 1984). Although a certain amount of random motion relieves abject rigidity, it appears to be more a disorder than a normal form of activity. Thus we must remove the "stiffness" of the computer graphic body to enhance the realism of synthesized human motion. There is reason to believe that such motions do not follow from random functions of joint angles, but rather appear from quasi-regular patterns of higher-level motions and goals. While quietly sitting, for example, a person still breathes, moves her head, touches her face, flexes her finger, shifts her feet, and so on. These motions are not due to totally random events, but imply that some component of indirectness is achieved by certain groups of motions with no ostensible goal (for example, scratching, fidgeting, doodling, foot shuffling, gazing, etc). This point of view could integrate natural motion cycles (gait Girard & Maciejewski, 1985), gestural cycles (eating, breathing), and positioning cycles (nervousness). Repetitious motion under these conditions must be more fully investigated.

Muscle tension and the flow parameter

For an individual body joint, forces are characterized by the flow dimension which may be taken as the overall muscle tension or friction at a joint, varying from no tension (free) to maximum tension (bound). Until recently, graphical animation systems (as well as our original simulation (Badler et al., 1980)) implemented maximum tension since no external (gravitational) or internal (inertial) forces can alter the prescribed path. By incorporating the ability to vary forces and muscle tension in a simulation, we can better model more realistic reaction to external forces.

One way to accomplish an effect like flow is to feed back through a "flow valve" the computed position and velocity of the limb end (based on the specified path) modified by the current set of active forces (Fig. 3.2). Bound movements correspond to a closed valve, hence no adjustment of the computed position. This is the usual computer graphics animation approach. A fully open valve ("free") corresponds to the forces acting on the limb end as if it

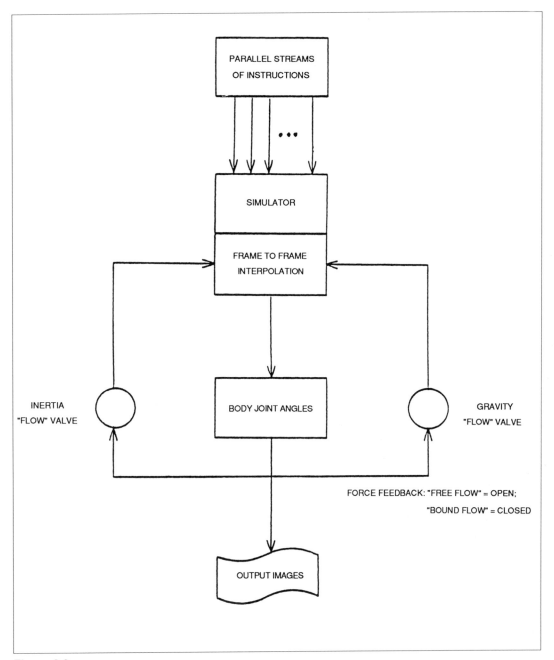

Figure 3.2
Adding Flow "valves" to the simulation process.

were in free fall, that is, with essentially no muscle tension opposing it. In between values create a mix of the two cases, and, hopefully, more natural movements.

Actually we believe that two independent valves are necessary: one to feed back inertial forces generated by the mass of the limb and another to feed back external loads (gravity or held objects) on the limb. Robot arm motion equations separate these forces explicitly (Hollerbach, 1983). The valve outputs are combined vectorially to determine the next position of the limb, that is, the result of feedback is a displacement vector times the "gravity" valve opening plus another displacement vector times the "inertial" valve opening. An example of this kind of situation might be holding a brick in the air. Vertical movements against gravity are relatively bound, otherwise the brick would fall. Sideways movements, however, may be more free since the inertia of the hand in a horizontal plane would be more difficult to overcome. Empirical data and arm dynamics formulations verify the separability of the two cases and show that the joint torques may be linearly combined (Atkeson & Hollerbach, 1984).

There is an implication of the flow factor for a motion representation used for simulation. Until recently, most animations were of the bound type; that is, motions were constrained to achieve key parameter values, to follow specific paths, or to implement discrete position or angle changes. Now there are several efforts (Wilhelms, 1987; Armstrong et al., 1987) to program actual dynamics formulations in order to synthesize motions which are based on internal or external forces. If there were there no resistance in the limb joints, the motion generated by external forces would appear to be unopposed by joint friction or muscle-induced internal resistive forces, and would therefore appear free. The connection between the two poles of animation techniques seems to be the flow factor. If we view dynamics simulation and key parameter techniques as simply two ends of a motion description scale, then motion effects which fall in the midrange can be achieved by combining the results of both schemes through the flow valves. In the case of tree-like articulated structures (such as the human body, if positioned without closed loops or connections to itself or the environment), Armstrong and Green (1987) have shown that the dynamics computation can be nearly done in real-time. Thus the overhead involved in computing both kinetic and dynamic motion descriptions may not significantly increase simulation cost.

Wilhelms (1987) simulates kinematic constraints with repulsive forces, for example, from the floor. For locomotion, Girard (1985) simulates dynamics first and then applies kinematic constraints such as joint limits. In practice it should be possible to compute both kinetics and dynamics concurrently and choose the flow-combined result as appropriate to the environment. For example, if an arm motion (such as a punch) must achieve a certain position of the fist, and the necessary forces to achieve the exact dynamics are not really known, then a guess could be made and the result biased by relatively bound flow in order to arrive at the final position with a reasonable expectation of accuracy. Alternatively, if the effect of an energetic punch with more upper torso involvement is expected, then the result can be biased by relatively free flow. The goal position may be exceeded, but that may be what was expected.

One result of using both kinetics and true dynamics is a blurring of the concept of motion duration required by the motion representation discussed so far. Since duration implies goal achievement, biasing a motion toward the dynamics computation should decrease the viability of strict temporal goals. Thus as the motion quality becomes more dynamics- dependent, duration must be sacrificed to more "environmental" constraints such as joint limits, body balance, obstacles, etc. Anyone who has tried to use the physical equations of motion to solve for a particular force or acceleration needed to reach a certain goal at a designated time can appreciate why such control is difficult to achieve by more intuitive (interactive) means (Wilhelms & Barsky, 1985). It is not surprising, then, that our original motion representation omitted durations from contact instructions: there was no way in advance to notate (hence describe) when the motions necessary to achieve a particular contact were to be initiated; rather, the contact was a modifier which assumed that the points in question were brought into proximity by other instructions and the contact itself achieved by simple heuristics and a pursuit algorithm (Badler et al., 1978; Badler et al., 1979; Badler et al., 1980).

There is an analogy between the flow quality and conventional animation techniques. In discussing Disney animation the distinction is drawn between straight ahead and pose to pose (Thomas & Johnston, 1981). We can compare pose to pose with key-parameter motion specification, and straight ahead to dynamics specification. Significantly, the terms used to describe the former are very close to those used to describe bound flow ("clarity," "strength," "control," "planned"), while those of the latter, free flow ("fresh," "zany," "funny," "spirited," "wild," "spontaneous"). Any particular action or sequence of actions, however, is likely to be a combination of the techniques refined to express the desired effect and varied over time to achieve a natural, animate texture (Thomas & Johnston, 1981), or uniquely human quality (Bartenieff, 1980).

Motion variation along a spatial path

The geometric form of the path of a body joint or a limb and effector may change as the rate of movement changes. We must allow control over the path to be independent of (or at least separable from) any kinetic control of velocity along the path. The path of a particle depends on its initial position, its velocity, and its (changing) acceleration. A weakness of Labanotation and, consequently, of our original motion representation, is the failure to provide specifics for motion parameters beyond average velocity (given implicitly by the duration and distances involved). To attempt a remedy, we look closely at definitions of the *weight* and *time* Effort qualities.

The weight factor spans light to strong qualities. Weight might first appear to imply a perceived mass of a limb or the body, but a more appropriate and computable interpretation is that the limb mass stays constant (or rather unknown and therefore not directly perceptible) and that weight refers to a more inertial quality such as "the mass resisted or moved by the limb." Consider this: from physics, force equals mass times acceleration. The total mass involved is the sum of both the internal (fixed) limb or body mass and the external mass moved. Since naive perception does not measure force directly, the total mass resisted or moved must be reflected in the acceleration (or deceleration) of the limb. Assuming the force exerted (say the maximum) is constant, the light quality may be achieved by increasing the acceleration to induce a perceived reduction in mass. Conversely, the strong Effort quality is conveyed by a decrease in acceleration and hence an increase in the perceived mass of the moved object. Evidence for this interpretation is based on two sources. The first is pantomime, where pushing a heavy block and a light block would be differentiated by the acceleration in the push: strong would involve a slow, deliberate motion, while light would appear as a quick action. Another example, easily verified, is the task of throwing balls of varying mass, such as a baseball and a shotput. The second source is the cinemagraphic technique of using slow motion to portray exceptional effort. When a performer swings a sword with all his might, and then another stroke is shown in slow motion, we get the impression that the latter is even stronger because the acceleration (in the slow time) is less. Thus the moved mass is greater. Since we do not see the mass actually increasing, we conclude that the force increased. Note that this is intuitively counter to the physics that would rather imply a decrease in acceleration yielding less force. The difference arises from mistaking the mass as that of the limb rather than the total "virtual" mass resisted, whether it be air or a real object.

The time Effort quality contributes additional information. To Bartenieff (1980) the time factor is related to some expected norm for the action. This interpretation is difficult to implement directly, so it is implied by controllable variation from a norm in any motion parameter. We take an alternative approach which concentrates instead on the rate of attack of a motion: Sustained time implies no change in velocity, that is, an acceleration of zero;

sudden implies a quick change in velocity, hence a rapid change in acceleration. We can justify this on two grounds:

• Arbitrarily assume that every primitive motion by itself starts at rest and ends at rest. Although all motions clearly do not act this way, we can use phrasing to combine motions and thereby create arbitrary motion transitions. Zero acceleration end conditions are a natural constraint and lend themselves to straightforward implementation (Steketee & Badler, 1985).

• The weight factor appears to function primarily at the terminus or decay of a motion where "force" is transferred to another object or projected into space.

These observations are satisfying for their symmetry. Whether they are valid is another matter. The way we will proceed to verify these interpretations of space, weight, and time (at least conceptually) is to consider the eight possible Effort combinations formed by taking the extremes of each factor (Table 3.2). The "action" column indicates whether goals or changes are the principal method of kinetic specification and also the relative rates of motion attack (acceleration) and decay (deceleration). The "work equivalent" is a convenient expression of the characteristics of a motion exhibiting extremes of each Effort quality. While it cannot be demonstrated here, performance of the eight motions according to the action, attack, and decay criteria will yield reasonable actions that fit understood semantics of the word equivalents.

While these examples do not have any absolute values associated with them, which makes relative comparisons difficult, it does appear that Effort time and weight provide qualitative acceleration information. Clearly the weight (force) information interacts (physically) with the mass of the moving limbs to determine the joint accelerations. Our challenge is to utilize this information in a fashion which avoids the significant calculations necessary for actual robotic control since our goal is, after all, graphical simulation. We may trade-off physical exactness for convincing motion quality. For instance, we may permit a slight shift in timing or a position correction from feedback near the end of a motion path as long as the "efforts" appear correct or appropriate. It is tantalizing to imagine that this situation is in fact obtained during the execution of unique or novel motion by a real person, and that repetition (practice) is necessary to actually iterate to complete achievement of all motion and timing constraints.

3 Effort Combinations Space-Time-Weight	Word Equiv.	Action (attack-decay)
direct-sudden-light	dabbing	goal, quick to quick
direct-sudden-strong	punching	goal, quick to slow
direct-sustained-light	gliding	goal, slow to quick
direct-sustained-strong	pressing	goal, slow to slow
indirect-sudden-light	flicking	change, quick to quick
indirect-sudden-strong	slashing	change, quick to slow
indirect-sustained-light	floating	change, slow to quick
indirect-sustained-strong	writhing	chance, slow to slow

Table 3.2
The eight extremes of the Effort qualities.

Implementation of Kinetic and Dynamic Control

By modeling paths as parametric curves (Faux & Pratt, 1979), both goals and path geometry may be represented and interpreted by the movement simulator. The use of polynomial curves to model (robot) end effector trajectories is not new (Paul, 1972; Herbison-Evans, 1978; Derby, 1983), nor is their use to model changing velocities and accelerations (Shelley & Greenberg, 1982; Sturman, 1984). The ability to control the tension in splines has also been used to vary animation kinetics (Kochanek, & Bartels, 1984; Emmett, 1985). Our studies have been directed toward more formal derivations of the form of these curves to generate movements with specific Effort qualities. The role of the animator is therefore moved to a higher level than just the manipulation of curves or their control points directly.

The basis for the implementation of the Effort qualities (as transformed into our "acceleration" conditions) is the double interpolant method of parametric interpolation (Steketee & Badler, 1985). The process of computing interpolated parameter values is divided into two steps: the first is a kinetic interpolation which maps times onto given keyframes, and the second is a position interpolation which maps the (transformed) keyframe times into actual parameter values. The result yields independent control over position and kinetics of the parameter along the "path" of keyframe values for that parameter, no matter what motion component that parameter actually controls.

To utilize the double interpolant method for the "Efforts," there must be a way of controlling the kinetic interpolant according to our acceleration analysis. For example, the default semantics of a path described by the kinetic interpolant might be equally-spaced keyframe times. Note that the other conditions imposed on the interpolation guarantee that there will be a smooth acceleration at the beginning and a smooth deceleration at the end. The rate of these changes is controllable, but the continuity is assured in any case. To effect the "dynamics" changes we alter the spacing of the keyframe times, that is, vary the "kinetic" interpolation. We do this by another interpolation which maps keyframe times onto keyframe times such that their order is preserved but their temporal spacing is altered.

The factors requiring control are exactly those cited above:

- attack acceleration at start of motion

- decay deceleration at end of motion

- true dynamic versus keyframe parameter control

- goals versus changes.

All of these vary along a single dimension, and are therefore amenable to control. The scheme we adopt is to treat the first and second as "infinite" scales, and the third and fourth as finite extremes. Thus the acceleration can be increased at the beginning and decreased at the end as much as desired. In the Hermite interpolation, this means that the slope of the keyframe to keyframe curve is varied from unity at the first knot to affect attack and at the last knot to affect decay. The slopes themselves are easily controlled by interactive graphical means if necessary. Moreover, the local control exhibited to our double interpolant implementation (as B-splines) permits local kinetic changes with a minimum of interaction or disturbance (Steketee & Badler, 1985).

The last two dimensions are also independent of the interpolations, as we have already discussed. Dynamic control may be needed mostly for fast movements since slow movements appear to be adequately controlled by path specification and kinetics (Vukobratovic & Stokie, 1983). If so, then it is not surprising that computer animation has worked best for relatively slow motions: the dynamics issue can be finessed by path control. When the motions become faster, dynamics can be expected to increase in importance and influence. It is no surprise then that much computer animation appears to have a lack of animacy, since slow motions eliminate more than half of the Effort terms in Table 3.1.

Movement Phrasing

Even though we can control an individual motion according to the dynamics parameters, real motions are grouped or phrased to smoothly blend a sequence of movements. Again the B-spline interpolated curves are useful here, as individual movements can be smoothly blended. The trick is not just to combine two motion curves, but to do so with a proper smoothing of the kinetics across the join. In particular, changes in the spatial path may be forced in the vicinity of the join (Steketee & Badler, 1985).

Rather than being a flow, the phrasing effect is real and is actually demonstrated in human motions. For example, phrasing occurs in a sequence of movements that can change over time as the performer becomes either more skilled and experienced, on the one hand, or more tired or rushed on the other. As has been observed in everyday discourse in both speech (Friedman, 1975) and American Sign Language (Klima & Bellugi, 1979; Frisberg, 1978), certain types of movements will be lost and others replaced with a related gesture towards the original target. Such changes are not derivable purely from the original movement specification, but require a sense of "fast speech" or "fast action" rules as well. The motion is not just faster along the phrased path, but the path itself is modified.

For a motion representation, the phrases must be indicated for every motion parameter. It is not viable to assume that all the human motions during some time period are phrased; rather, some motions may be phrased, others not, or the phrasing may overlap (Venable, 1983). Thus any symbolic realization of the motion representation must permit the specification of such arbitrary phrases in addition to the other motion qualities.

Higher Level Motion Constructs

For a long time we and others have searched for a means to express the higher-level relationships between motions such as concurrency, overlap, mutual exclusion, etc. In the movement "architecture" paradigm (Weber et al., 1978), we looked at languages defined on top of the primitives which would permit expression of repetitions, conditionals, and the like; others have tried more visual approaches such as track animation systems to control concurrency and parallelism (Feiner, Salesin, & Banchoff, 1982; Fortin, Lamy, & Thalmann, 1986; Gomez & Twixt, 1984). When simulation principles are introduced, relationships and interactions between entities are easier to control (Kahn & Hewitt, 1978; Magnenat-Thalmann & Thalmann, Oct., 1985). A major difficulty is that neither one- nor two-dimensional (graphical) languages provide comfortable structures with which to express these interlocking temporal and geometric relationships (Magnenat-Thalmann & Thalmann, 1985). The direction we are presently taking is to model the higher level control issues as just that: structures which represent explicitly the actions and their relationships.

We have three systems implementing such models:

1. The first is a facial animation system (OASIS) based on an object-oriented approach to motion control (Platt, 1985). Its salient features are the separation of actions, objects, and the application algorithm which maps specific actions onto specific objects. Though the

underlying motions may be defined parametrically, the control flow is organized by the allowable actions applied to objects, and the propagation of those actions or their consequential actions to other objects within the same instantaneous time. For facial animation, this system uses face regions with knowledge of their connections to other face regions. the facial actions know how to propagate across the region connection types.

2. The second is a hierarchical reasoning system (HIRES) which permits modeling a process or activity at multiple levels of detail or with differing representations. Though implemented as a production rule system, HIRES supports pre-processors for continuous system simulation models, discrete simulation models, petri nets, timed petri nets, and scripts. For example, an elevator simulation might be represented at the lowest level as a dynamics problem, that is, by modeling within a continuous system simulation paradigm; the next level might be a queuing system (discrete) model; while the upper levels can be symbolic, state-based, qualitative-reasoning models. A common knowledge base and mechanisms for moving up and down through the hierarchy of models is provided. The resulting simulation creates explicit motion parameters (say from the dynamics level) or parametric keyframes (from the discrete modeling levels). We have used HIRES to animate five human figures seated at a table eating according to the well-known "dining philosophers" problem in operating systems. The sequence and synchronization tasks are handled in HIRES; the motions are generated by the execution of the simulation at the desired process abstraction level. The eating process itself is modeled as a set of parametric keyframes derived from our human body positioning system TEMPUS (Badler et al., 1985). The simulation selects the appropriate keyframes according to the "rules" of the process description.

3. The third system, still under development, consists of a natural language interface and a knowledge base which encodes an understanding of some simple English verbs of motion (Gangel, 1985). The structure built from the input utterance is to be passed to HIRES for simulation. An extension to this system will use English verbs to characterize more complex activities and, in particular, incorporate the Effort extremes as they have tantalizing verb equivalents (Table 3.1). Using these factors and our implementation of their semantics as the core concepts of an animation system based on natural language input, we can imagine modeling particular actions by adverbial modifications of the closest motion verb (Tsotsos et al., 1980). The linear nature of the representation scales demonstrated above is well-suited to linguistic adverbial modifications much as more or less of some character. These concepts appear to come much closer to the expressiveness or intent of an action than the spatial descriptions of Labanotation, graphical languages, or robot control systems. Work on a high level animation system where actions are sketched out (like a storyboard) and modified through these language concepts is underway.

The point of these systems is to control the animation process at descriptive levels appropriate to the process being controlled. Thus, as long as our figures or objects want to move in simple ways, simple techniques will suffice. As soon as we expect natural, fluid, coordinated, task-oriented, and expressive motions, the control systems become more important, increase in complexity, and move beyond the computer graphics domain into simulation and artificial intelligence.

Conclusions

The need for better animation control is apparent from the literature. The qualitative factors of Effort-Shape notation have been used to suggest extensions to existing movement representations in directions consistent with known characteristics of human movement and conventional animation. We have shown how the Effort motion qualities may be at least approximated by a combination of kinetics and dynamics computations, with kinetic control modulated by acceleration and decelerations derived from existing interpolation methods. In addition, the interactions between two motions by phrasing may be handled explicitly by modifications expressed in the representation. Temporal, spatial, and relationship interactions may be described and executed within an appropriately detailed model.

Checking the motion representation proposed here against the criteria set forth at the beginning of this discussion, we can verify that it meets all of them:

- The representation has *descriptive significance* because the abstractions of position, motion and dynamics based on Labanotation and Effort notation permit comparison between motion descriptions independent of the source. It should not matter, for example, whether attack and decay values have been obtained through direct sensor measurements, mathematical functions, or human interactive design. Nor should it be particularly special that the attack and decay values are used for animation; they could just as well be used as the basis for natural language descriptions of the quality of the motion.

- The representation admits *modifiability through generally accessible methods* since there are straightforward controls over each descriptive type. The motion specification consists primarily of joint angle changes, Cartesian reach goals, and sequences of points in suitable parameter spaces. Control of these is typically based on interactive systems (for example, (Badler et al., 1985; Sturman, 1984). The kinetics and dynamics specification extends the set to four scales with relatively natural interpretations and significance of values along the scales. An interactive system could have "potentiometers" for each factor. Language appears to have such control already built in using adverbial modifiers such as more and less. In either situation artistic ability does not appear to dominate the motion specification or modification task, since the factors can be adjusted easily.

- The representation is *independent of specific individuals* since there is a strong inclusion of goals which are achieved as allowed by the individual model's anthropometry (Korein, 1985). In addition, the dynamics description mechanism does not necessarily require specific characteristics of an individual's musculature. Although this may make it more difficult to duplicate the motions of a particular individual, it should be easier to produce (by refinement) a particular motion effect on any arbitrarily-sized human figure.

- Finally, the representation demonstrates *independence of specific motion characteristics*. Any of the kinetic or dynamics factors may be varied independently of the others. All of the motion factors are independent of particular body positions. This does not mean that the appearance of every combination of values allowed by the representation will be unique, but only that each factor may be separately manipulated for localized experimentation. Furthermore, since all motion factors can be represented by values on the four scales, they can be parameterized. Motion joining, smoothing, and phrasing is extended to the dynamics cases as well. Several animation systems are running or are under development at the University of Pennsylvania to demonstrate the feasibility and efficacy of these approaches. We are anxious to experiment with them and produce animations showing processes involving the interaction of several people with a complexity not yet demonstrated elsewhere.

Acknowledgements

This investigation has been greatly aided by discussions with many colleagues and students, especially Bonnie Webber, Jim Korein, Jon Korein, Steve Platt, Paul Fishwick, Scott Steketee, Diana Dadamo, Lisa Koelewyn, David Cebula, and Jeffrey Esakov. Moral support from Ann Hutchinson Guest on issues of dynamics and Effort-Shape Notation is much appreciated. This research is partially supported by NASA Contract NAS9-17239, Lockheed Engineering and Management Services, NSF CER Grant MCS-82-19196, NSF Grants IST-86-12984 and DMC-85-16114, and ARO Grant DAAAG29-84-K-0061 including participation by the U.S. Army Human Engineering Laboratory.

References

Akita, K. (1982). Analysis of body motion image sequences. *Proceedings of the 6th International Conference on Pattern Recognition*. 320–327.

Allen, J. (1984). Towards a general theory of action and time. *Artificial Intelligence, 23,* 2.

Armstrong, W., Green, M., & Lake, R. (1987). Near-real-time control of human figure models. *IEEE Computer Graphics and Applications 7, 6,* 52–61.

Atkeson, C., & Hollerbach, J. (1984). Kinematic features of unrestrained arm movements. *A. I. Memo 790,* Artificial Intelligence Lab, MIT, Cambridge, MA.

Badler, N. (1975). *Temporal scene analysis: Conceptual descriptions of object movement.* Unpublished doctoral thesis, Department of Computer Science, The University of Toronto, Canada.

Badler, N., Smoliar, S., O'Rourke, J., & Webber, L. (1978). *The simulation of human movement.* Unpublished paper, Department of Computer Science, The University of Toronto, Canada.

Badler, N., O'Rourke, J., Platt, S., & Morris, M. (1980). Human movement understanding: A variety of perspectives. *Proceedings of the AAAI Conference,* Stanford, California, 53–55.

Badler, N., Webber, B., Korein, J. D., & Korein, J. U. (1983). TEMPUS, a system for the design and simulation of mobile agents in a workstation and task environments. *Proceedings of the IEEE Trends and Applications Conference,* 263–269.

Badler, N., Korein, J.D., Korein, J.U., Radack, G., & Brotman L. (1985). Positioning and animating human figures in a task-oriented environment. *The Visual Computer: The International Journal of Computer Graphics,* 1(4), 212–220.

Badler, N., & Bajcsy, R. (1978). Three-dimensional representations for computer graphics and computer vision. *Computer Graphics,* 2(3), 153–160.

Badler, N., & Smoliar, S. (1979). Digital representation of human movement. *ACM Computing Surveys,* 11(1), 19–38.

Badler, N., O'Rourke, J. & Kaufman, B. (1980). Special problems in human movement simulation. *Computer Graphics,* 14(3), 189–197.

Baecker, R. (1969). Picture driven animation. *Proceedings of the AFIPS Spring Joint Conference.* Montvale, New Jersey: AFIPS Press, 273–288.

Bartenieff, I. (1980). *Body movement: Coping with the environment.* New York: Gordon and Breach.

Burtnyk, N., & Wein, M. (1976). Interactive skeleton techniques for enhancing motion dynamics in key frame animation. *Communication of the ACM,* 19(10), 564–569.

Calvert, T., Chapman, J., & Patla, A. (1980). The integration of subjective and objective data in the animation of human movement. *Computer Graphics,* 14(3), 198–203.

Calvert, T., Chapman, J., & Patla, A. (1982). Aspects of the kinematic simulation of human movement. *IEEE Computer Graphics and Applications, 2*(9), 41–50.

Catmull, E. (1972). A system for computer generated movies. *Proceedings of the ACM Annual Conference,* 422–431.

Clark, J. (1976). Hierarchical geometric models for visible surface algorithms. *Communication of the ACM, 19*(10), 547–554.

Dell, C. (1970). *A Primer for movement description.* New York: Dance Notation Bureau.

Derby, S. (1983). Simulating motion elements of general-purpose robot arm. *International Journal of Robotics Research, 2*(1), 3–12.

Emmett, A. (1985). Digital portfolio: Tony de Peltrie. *Computer Graphics World, 8*(10), 72–77.

Faux, I., & Pratt, M. (1979). *Computational geometry for design and manufacture.* Chichester, England: Ellis Horwood.

Feiner, S., Salesin, D., & Banchoff, T. (1982), Dial: A diagrammatic animation language. *IEEE Computer Graphics and Applications, 2*(7), 43–54.

Fishwick, P. (1986). *Hierarchical reasoning: Simulating complex processes over multiple levels of abstraction.* Unpublished doctoral thesis, Department of Computer Science, The University of Pennsylvania, Philadelphia.

Fortin, D., Lamy, J.F., & Thalman, D. (1986). A multiple track animator for motion synchronization. In N. I. Badler & J.K. Tsotsos (Eds.) *Motion: Representation and perception.* New York: Elsevier, North Holland, 311–317.

Friedman, J. (1975). Computer exploration of fast speech rules. *IEEE Trans on Accoustics, Speech, and Signal Processing, 23*(1), 100–103.

Frisberg, N. (1978). The case of the missing length. *Communication and Cognition, 11*(1), 57–67.

Gangel, J. (1985). *A motion verb interface to a task animation system.* Unpublished master's thesis, Department of Information and Computer Science, The University of Pennsylvania.

Ginsberg, C., & Maxwell, D. (1986). Graphical marionette. In N. I. Badler & J. K. Tsotsos, (Eds.), *Motion: Representation and Perception.* New York: Elsevier, North Holland, 303–310.

Girard, M., & Maciejewski, A. (1985). Computational modeling for the computer animation of legged figures. *Computer Graphics, 19*(3), 263–270.

Girard, M. (1987). Interactive design of 3-D computer-animated legged animal motion. *IEEE Computer Graphics and Applications, 7*(6), 39–51.

Gomez, J. (1984). Twixt: A 3-D animation system. *Proceedings of Eurographics '84,* 121–133.

Herbison-Evans, D., & Richardson, D. (1981). Control of round-off propagation in articulating the human figure. *Computer Graphics and Image Processing, 12*(3), 386–393.

Herbison-Evans, D. (1978). NUDES2: A numeric utility displaying ellipsoid solids. *Computer Graphics, 12*(3), 354–356.

Hollerbach, J. (1980). A recursive lagrangian formulation of manipulator dynamics and a comparative study of dynamics formulation complexity. *IEEE Trans. Systems, Man, and Cybernetics, 10*(11), 730–736.

Hutchinson, A. (1970). *Labanotation.* New York: Theater Arts Books.

Kahn, K., & Hewitt, C. (1978). Dynamic graphics using quasi-parallelism. *Computer Graphics, 12*(3), 357–362.

Klima, E., & Bellugi, U. (1979). *The signs of language.* Cambridge, MA: Harvard University Press.

Kochanek, D., & Bartels, R. (1984). Interpolating splines with local tension, continuity, and bias control. *Computer Graphics, 18*(3), 33–41.

Korein, J., & Badler, N. (1983). Temporal anti-aliasing in computer generated animation. *Computer Graphics, 17*(3), 377–388.

Korein, J. (1985). *A geometric investigation of reach.* Cambridge, MA: MIT Press.

Korein, J., & Badler, N. (1982). Techniques for goal directed motion. *IEEE Computer Graphics and Applications, 2*(9), 71–81.

Lee, H.J., & Chen, Z. (1985). Determination of 3D human body postures from a single view. *Computer Vision, Graphics and Image Processing, 30*(2), 148–168.

Linehan, T. (1985). Ohio State pioneers computer animation. *Computer Graphics World, 8*(10), 46–60.

Loomis, J., Poizner, H., Bellugi, U., Blakemore, A., & Hollerbach, J. (1983). Computer graphic modeling of American Sign Language. *Computer Graphics, 17*(3), 105–114.

Lozano-Perez, T., & Wesley, M. (1979), An algorithm for planning collision-free paths among polyhedral obstacles. *Communication of the ACM, 22*(10), 560–570.

Magnenat-Thalman, N., & Thalman, D. (1985). Three-dimensional computer animation: More an evolution than a motion problem. *IEEE Computer Graphics and Applications, 5*(10), 47–57.

Magnenat-Thalman, N., & Thalman, D. (1985). *Computer animation.* New York: Springer-Verlag.

Mandlebrot, B. (1977). *Fractals: Form, chance, and dimension.* San Francisco: Freeman.

Marr, D., & Nishihara, H. (1981). Representation and recognition of the spatial organization of three-dimensional shapes. *Proceedings of the Royal Society.* London: B200.

Mezei, L., & Zivian, A. (1971). ARTA, an interactive animation system. *Proceedings of the IFIP Congress,* 429–434.

Michotte, A. (1946). *La perception do la causalite.* Paris: Louvain.

Miller, G. (1972). English verbs of motion: A case study in semantics and lexical memory. In A. W. Melon & E. Martin (Eds,) *Coding processes in human memory.* Washington, DC: V. H. Winston & Sons, 335–372.

O'Rourke, J., & Badler, N. (1980). Model-based image analysis of human motion using constraint propogation. *IEEE Trans, PAMI, 2*(6), 522–536.

Parke, F. (1982). Parameterized models for facial animation. *IEEE Computer Graphics and Animation, 2*(9), 61–68.

Paul, R. (1981). *Robot manipulators: Mathematics, programming, and control.* Cambridge, MA: MIT Press.

Paul, R. (1972). Modeling, trajectory calculation and servicing of a computer controlled arm. *Stanford AI Project Memo, 177.*

Paul, R. (1979). Manipulator cartesian path control. *IEEE Trans. Systems, Man, and Cybernetics, 9*(11), 702–711.

Platt, S., & Badler, N. (1981). Animating facial expression. *Computer Graphics, 15*(3), 245–252.

Platt, S., (1985). *A structural model of the human face.* Unpublished doctoral thesis, Department of Computer and Information Science, The University of Pennsylvania.

Reeves, W. (1981). Inbetweening for computer animation utilizing moving point constraints. *Computer Graphics, 15*(3), 263–269.

Reeves, W. (1983). Particle systems—a technique for modelling a class of fuzzy objects. *Computer Graphics, 17*(3), 359–376.

Reeves, W. (1985). Approximate and probabilistic algorithms for shading and rendering structured particle systems. *Computer Graphics, 19*(3), 313–322.

Schank, R. (1975). Conceptual information processing. Amsterdam: North Holland.

Shelley, K., & Greenberg, D. (1982). Path specification and path coherence. *Computer Graphics, 16*(3), 157–166.

Steketee, S., & Badler, N. (1985). Parametric keyframe interpolation incorporating kinetic adjustment and phrasing control. *Computer Graphics, 19*(3), 255–262.

Sturman, D. (1984). Interactive key frame animation of 3-D articulated models. *Proceedings of Graphics Interface '84.* Ottawa, Canada, 35–40.

Thomas, F., & Johnston, O. (1981). *Disney animation: The illusion of life*. New York: Abbeville Press.

Tsotsos, J., Mylopoulos, J., Covvey, H., & Zucker, S. (1980). A framework for visual motion understanding. *IEEE Trans, PAMI, 2*(6), 563-573.

Venable, L. (1983), 1983 I.C.L.L. Conference report. *Dance Notation Journal, 1*(2), 30–32.

Vere, S. (1983). Planning in time: Windows and durations for activities and goals. *IEEE Trans. on Pattern Analysis and Maching Intelligence, 5*(3), 246–267.

Vukobratovic, M., & Stokic, D. (1983). Is dynamic control needed in robotic systems, and if so, to what extent? *International Journal of Robotics Research, 2*(2), 18–34.

Waltz, D. (1982). Event shape diagrams. *Proceedings of AAAI-82*, 84–87.

Weber, l., Smoliar, S., & Badler, N. (1978). An architecture for the simulation of human movement. *Proceedings of Graphics Interface '85*, Montreal, 97–104.

Wilhelms, J., & Barsky B. (1985). Using dynamics for the animation of articulated bodies such as humans and robots. *Proceedings of Graphics Interface '85*, Montreal, 97–104

Wilhelms, J. (1987). Using dynamic analysis for realistic animation of articulated bodies. *IEEE Computer Graphics and Applications, 7*(6), 12–27.

Wilhelms, J. (1987). Toward automatic motion control. *IEEE Computer Graphics and Applications, 7*(4), 11–22.

Zeltzer, D. (1986). Knowledge-based animation. In N. I. Badler & J. K. Tsotsos (Eds.) *Motion: Representation and perception*. New York: Elsevier, North Holland.

Zeltzer, D. (1982). Motor control techniques for figure animation. *IEEE Computer Graphics and Applications, 2*(9), 53–59.

4 Programming a Robot to Dance

Margo K. Apostolos
University of Southern California
Los Angeles, California

Robot choreography was developed to explore the aesthetic implications of robotic movement. Initially, this research began with the question, "Can a robot dance?" The investigation of this question resulted in the development of a technique to program an industrial robotic arm to move in an aesthetic fashion (Apostolos, 1984). This chapter will present the development of robot choreography and examine the aesthetic implications of robotic movement.

Robotic Movement

A robot is typically used to perform utilitarian tasks as designated by specific computer programs. The "work" of the robot is often characterized by efficient, staccato-type movement sequences which are devised from the viewpoint of efficiency rather than immediate aesthetic appeal. Robot motion that is designed to be functionally efficient is not always aesthetically pleasing. This fact is believed to be an important negative factor in the consideration of user acceptance of robotic devices.

Choreographic Approach

The purpose of this research was to explore the aesthetic elements of robotic movement based on a choreographic approach. A combined effort works to integrate the sounds of music, the forms of sculpture, and the motions of dance. Choreography, the art of making dances, uses dance as a series of rhythmic motions in time and space to express ideas through movement. The connotation of dance and choreography suggest direct human involvement or participation in the movement sequences; hence the very idea of a robot dancing may seem self-contradictory. The human element is involved in the programming of movement sequences for the robot; however, a "dancing" robot or robot "choreography" may be used only as metaphors. The process of choreographing for a robotic arm combines a logical approach with a sensuous approach in a blend of artistic-scientific creativity.

The idea of "dehumanized dance" is not entirely new; many of the works of American choreographer Alwin Nikolais were based on this concept. The Nikolais dancers moved in a mechanical style, virtually stripped of their human identity through technical effects. The dancers were manipulated through space and time by the controls of this master choreographer. Nikolais' work was strongly influenced by the Bauhaus School of Design (Mazo, 1977).

As part of this work, an attempt was made to present movement of a robotic arm in the form of choreographed sequences of robotic movement synchronized with music. The mechanical features of the staccato action of the robotic arm are contrasted with what has been defined as "aesthetic maneuvers." The aesthetic movements feature a more sustained effort in the actions, smoother transitions from point to point, curved lines replacing many of the straight and short angular motions, and a varied sequence in the timing of movement phrases to break up the constant speed characteristic of the practical patterns of robot movement. The aesthetic maneuvers explore the related movement elements of the action quality, flow, shape, and timing in various movement phrases.

Movement elements often used in dance choreography are used in the design of robot tasks. The elements of shape, space, time, and force are used in dance exploration, and these movement elements can be used in dance exploration, and in application to robot tasks. The position and actual movements of the robot in vertical and horizontal planes comprise the basis for shape exploration. Space is a factor which further distinguishes movement by direction, dimension, level, path, and focus. The rate of speed (tempo) of the movement, and the subsequent rhythmic pattern of motion are paramount concerns in the development of aesthetic sequences of robotic movement. The elements of force, i.e., energy, effort, weight, and dynamics relates to the intensity of movement.

The quality of movement then results when time, tempo, and intensity are treated in certain relations to both gravity and space. The primary movement qualities commonly identified in dance studies are percussive, sustained, and pendular with corresponding secondary qualities of vibratory, suspension, and collapse. These six qualities of movement, which are based on the elements of shape, space, time, and force are used in the development of an aesthetic mode for common robot "work" tasks.

The Bauhaus School of Design

The creative process of industrial design combines the artistic impression of the designer with actual production of utilitarian objects. The union of the artist and the craftsman at the Bauhaus School of Design was exemplified with the manifesto: Art and Technology—A New Unity. The interaction of man and machine was an important concern of this German design school. The Bauhaus School developed a way of creative thinking and problem solving with relation to the working environment. The combination of art and technology was more than the isolated work of art or the isolated work of technology (Wingler, 1969).

Actually, the notion of "robot choreography" may not adhere strictly to the aesthetic concerns of the Bauhaus designers. At the Bauhaus, the beauty of the robot may have been found to be the naked form of the device moving with mechanical, sharp, and staccato actions. Thus, the application of synchronized robotic movement may be contrary to Bauhaus thought.

Kinetic Art

The kinetic arts have emerged from a union of artistic ideas and technological advances. Kinetic art includes two and three dimensional works in actual movement; i.e. machines, projections, and works in virtual movement which rely on the spectator's eye responding to a physical stimulus (Popper, 1968).

The strongest influence in the development of kinetic art has come from the science and technology sphere. The idea of the wheel, fireworks, fountains, mechanical mobiles, and robots are examples of the influence of technology. The kinetic artist began working in a new medium, although various artistic traits can apply to the design of both art and technology. These traits include craftsmanship, conceptional-visual thinking, and design which are important factors to consider in the development and analysis of choreographed robotic movement.

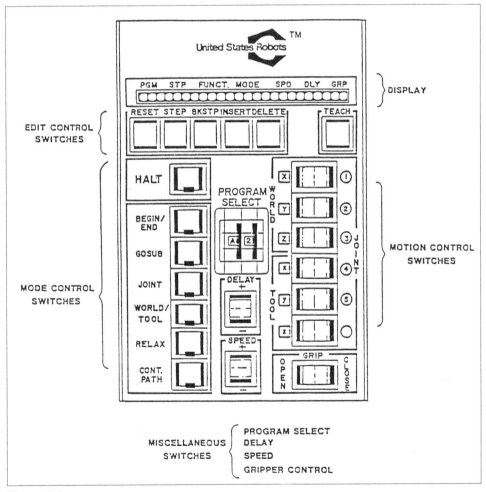

Figure 4.1
The U.S. Robot Teach Pendant from the U.S. Robot Programming Manual.

Movement Notation

The need for a universal movement notation system to assist in programming robot movement is a salient feature in the future development of robot choreography. Currently, "dance steps" for the robots have been adapted within the available programming languages; i.e. the Unimation PUMA robots are operated through VAL and VALII, the Spine robots and the U.S. Robot are programmed with system specific languages. Much of the programming can be done through a teach pendant (see Figure 4.1) which controls the movement of the robotic manipulator. The movement notation system that I have created is user specific and not easily interpreted. A natural language interface would be most desirable in the programming of robot choreography.

```
              PROGRAM box
1             SPEED 40 ALWAYS
2             MOVE #bx1
3             DELAY 1
4             SPEED 50
5             MOVE #bx1a
6             MOVE #bx2
7             MOVE #bx3
8             MOVE #bx4
9             MOVE #bx5
10            MOVE#bx6
11            RETURN
```

Figure 4.2
Example of a program for the Unimation PUMA 560.

A program for robot choreography consists of various routines and sub-routines. Individual points are named and recorded as movement points in space. These points are linked together into movement phrases which constitute the sub-routines and routines. An example of a program for the Unimation PUMA 560 written in VALII, is illustrated in Figure 4.2.

The points in space have been designated by the terms #bx1, #bx1a, etc., while the speeds (40 and 50) are relative to the system speed. The DELAY 1 represents a delay of 1 second in real time. Most of my programming and choreography is done from the joint mode; that is,

	Jt1	Jt2	Jt3	Jt4	Jt5	Jt6
#bx1	3.351	11.360	-9.794	89.478	84.666	-54.74
#bx1a	0.011	-90.011	90.000	-0.011	-52.053	-0.02
#bx2	3.351	-178.595	173.595	-91.681	-82.392	-152.97
#bx3	159.774	-137.104	-14.073	-91.681	5.641	-95.49
#bx4	157.841	-137.109	-48.098	-2.252	-95.142	6.31
#bx5	-9.393	137.011	-48.098	-2.252	-95.142	6.31
#bx6	0.000	-90.006	90.000	-0.005	-0.005	-0.01

Figure 4.3
The PROGRAM box point positions.

by manipulating each joint of the robot independently. This particular program (box) can be linked to other programs which would comprise a master routine.

Individual points in space are recorded with reference to joint angles. Most of the robots that I have worked with are manipulated by six degrees of freedom. The degrees of freedom refer to specific joints on the limb; i.e. shoulder rotation—joint 1, shoulder flexion and extension—joint 2, elbow flexion and extension—joint 3, wrist rotation—joint 4, end effector flexion and extension—joint 5, and end effector rotation—joint 6. These joint positions are stored within the system and recorded with the point names indicated in the programs. For example, the PROGRAM box point positions are stored as indicated by Figure 4.3.

The joint angles are in the system's memory which are relative to the robot's calibrated position. The robot positions are calculated in reference to the calibrated position. Calibration is generally held in vertical upright position, although the robot systems do vary.

A Final Note

The impact of a collaboration between art and technology is pronounced in this era of advanced technology. The development of computer music, computer graphics, and robot choreography reflects this technological influence. The increase and assimilation of robots in society coupled with the issue of user acceptance and the user/machine interface will warrant further investigation into the aesthetic implications of robotic movement.

References

Apostolos, M. (1984). *Exploring user acceptance of a robotic arm: A multidisciplinary case study.* Unpublished doctoral dissertation, Stanford University.

Mazo, J. (1977). *Prime Movers.* New York: William Morrow and Company Inc., 26.

Wingler, H. (1969). *The Bauhaus.* Cambridge, MA: The M.I.T. Press, 52.

Popper, F. (1968). *Origins and developments of kinetic art*, New York: New York Graphic Society, 105.

5 The Use of a Motion Detector in Dance Instruction and Performance

Alice Trexler and Ronald K. Thornton
Tufts University
Medford, Massachusetts

Microcomputer-based laboratory (MBL) tools allow students to gather data on physical phenomena such as motion, using inexpensive probes connected to a microcomputer. The microcomputer is programmed to display the data in graphical form as it is being collected. In this chapter, the authors have developed aesthetic applications for one such tool. A motion detector already in use in science laboratories is being adapted for use in dance instruction and performance.

The Motion Detector

A description of the motion detector will make its application to dance much clearer. The motion detector (which was developed at Technical Education Research Centers (TERC) under a National Science Foundation grant) makes use of a sonic transducer used in Polaroid cameras. The detector sends out short pulses of high frequency sound far above the range of human hearing and detects the echo (much the same way a bat locates objects). A microcomputer is used to measure the time between the transmission and received pulse, and then to calculate the position, velocity, and acceleration of the object causing the reflection. Any or all of these quantities can be graphed simultaneously on the computer monitor. The detector senses the nearest object in roughly a 30 degree cone and measures the motion along a line connecting the motion detector and the object. For our work we will be using motion detectors coupled to Apple computers.

Choreography in the Physics Laboratory

The motion detector is being successfully used in science labs for students of the arts and humanities at Tufts University. As students move their own bodies they are able to understand concepts related to motion and to watch the symbolic representation of their motion—graphs of position, velocity, and acceleration over time—being formed on the screen. Among other activities, students are asked to reproduce graphs included in written laboratory materials by moving in an appropriate way. To follow such specific movement instructions (a simple choreographic notation), students must be able to interpret the graphs and act on their interpretation by moving correctly. The authors of this paper are excited by the idea of extending the use of the motion detector from the physics laboratory to the movement realm of dance performance and dance instruction.

As part of this physics lab, students are asked to walk toward and away from the detector in straight and irregular lines. In some exercises, they must also retard and accelerate their movement. In such a laboratory students are able to link the concrete measurement of a physical system to the simultaneous production of its symbolic representation. Their movement paths and patterns are dictated by the restraints of the laboratory problems that the instructor provides. A few of the lab problems actually "performed" by physics students are shown in Figure 5.1. Since an understanding of the physical world is a major goal, any aesthetic considerations are incidental.

Cross-Disciplinary Dance Education

One philosophy of education in the arts and in science is that students learn best by studying the works of "great masters." For example, students in the science lab are often required to reproduce well-known experiments, whereas many dance composition students are required to view the choreography of recognized professionals. The authors of this paper believe that immersion in process is an equally important avenue to education and that students often learn best by involvement in their own and in their peers' creations.

The use of the motion detector can facilitate cross-disciplinary dance education whether by physics students learning aesthetic concepts as a by-product of studying physical laws or dance students learning physics as a by-product of their creative problem solving with movement. Furthermore, the interaction of two collaborators from different fields offers new insights into the creative process.

With only a small leap of the imagination, the choreographer and dance educator can begin to envision aesthetic applications of the technology used for science labs in performance and dance class settings. But since movement and stillness are the material of choreography, even physics students with no dance training can be instructed to design floor patterns with walking while accomplishing objective goals with the equipment. The possibilities of pauses and changes of tempo provide other variables that can be played with to create seemingly endless variations on the theme of walking. (Note that even a change in terminology—"floor patterns," "pause," "tempo," "theme"—brings an artistic intent into an otherwise objective laboratory experience.) So, if science students can attend to and learn about simple aesthetic concepts through experimentation in a laboratory, students integrating technology with choreography can be directed to experiment with such objective aspects of the physical world as measurement and its symbolic representation. Most importantly, the manipulation of unfamiliar technological devices by dance students can open a wealth of creative problems (such as those in the description of the performance later).

The motion detector has been used as a learning tool by dance composition students at Tufts University. This laboratory work has been divided into four sections:

1. Selected physics lab problems such as those shown in Figure 5.1 (The students must understand the relationship of their movement to the screen display and the different modalities of the motion—position, velocity, and acceleration).

2. Creative movement problems that produce random graphic results:

• Example 1: Improvise with arms slowly while moving quickly toward and away from the detector.

3. Make a distance graph walking medium fast away from the detector and then medium fast toward the detector. Sketch the graph.

a. Make a velocity graph walking slowly and steadily away from the detector. Sketch the result here.

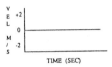

5. Draw below your prediction of the graph if a person:

   a) Starts at the 1-meter mark, walks steadily and slowly away, stops for four seconds, and then walks quickly back.

   b) Compare predictions. See if you can all agree.

   c) Do the experiment and repeat until you find an answer that seems correct.

   d) Draw your group's final result on the second graph.

   Note: Put in the time and distance scale.

PREDICTION   FINAL RESULT

4. Make a graph that looks like the wave pattern shown below. Try to get the times right and the speeds right.

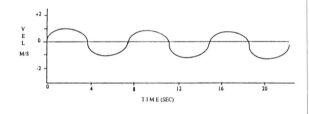

8. Move to make a curved line graph like the one below

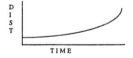

Describe a rule for making such a graph.

_____

_____

_____

Figure 5.1
Selected exercises from the motion laboratory.

- Example 2: Improvise freely moving in and out of the detector's range, both near and far from the detector.

    3. Graphs as simplistic notation

- Example l: Improvise movement that will create a predetermined graph.

- Example 2: Make a simple distance graph with walking and duplicate it with improvised movement.

    4. Intentional graphic design by the dancer

- Example l: What body movement produces straight lines? jagged lines? fussy lines?

- Example 2: Draw a graph on paper including several design variables. Approximate this graph on the screen by moving appropriately.

Parts 3 and 4 of the lab illustrate processes that require a sophisticated and integrative intellectual process by the student. A great deal of practice is required to improvise movement that will closely approximate a display of changing velocities or positions over a period of seconds. This process requires that the graph act as a crude notation. Even when each graphic (notation) deals with only one aspect of the movement over time (position, velocity, or acceleration), the notation is so specific in this aspect that reproducing the motion can be quite challenging.

The movement notation system termed "labanotation" includes a scheme called "motif writing" which is, like the graphs we have been discussing, an incomplete form of notation that can be carried out with improvised movement. However, motif writing does not demand the same high degree of specificity in any of its aspects as does the graphic notation in particular aspects. Because of this specificity, strategies for creating different design variables must be practiced by the dancer using the detector's simultaneously produced graphs as feedback. Furthermore, creating a curved or jagged velocity graph, for example, will require different movements than creating the same designs using a position graph. In addition, since bodies cannot move from one point to another in zero time, straight vertical lines can be made on the position graph only through the interaction of two or more people with the detector.

The computer-produced graphs that are a product of motion can also be aesthetic catalysts. The movement created by the dance or science students, for example, can be influenced solely by their interest in the visual design of the graphs, if they are so directed in the laboratory exercises. The graphs can also be used as a nonspecific kind of notation within which dancers improvise. Both the visual art possibilities of the graphs and the interaction of aesthetically manipulated motion with the detector and display have interested these authors in developing not only educational experiences, but also performance which interfaces new technology with dance.

Technology as a Choreographic Resource

Inexperienced dance students can sometimes create fresh approaches to dance, and technoprobes can sometimes envision new uses for technology. The latter was the case when the collaborators first began their work. The choreographer, with only a slight acquaintance with the motion detector, first envisioned the graphics as a changing decor for choreography. Next, plans for training dancers to control the graphics were discussed. Finally, a whole range of contrast devices for a composition emerged from speculative discussions (see next section) between the writers.

The motion detector itself was created for use in the science classroom. The scientist, although a nonartist, metaphorically considered the actions prescribed by the laboratory problems as a simple kind of choreography, which led him to think there might be fruitful connections to dance. The ensuing collaboration led to dance performance and teaching concepts that were not part of the motivating force behind the development of the motion detector. When this technology was placed in a "foreign" frame of reference, i.e. dance, new applications immediately surfaced, and even though the choreographer was at first unaware of the device's limitations, the list of interesting choreographic ideas grew so long that many were actually possible. The use of the motion detector with its limited but highly specific functions within the context of choreographic creativity provides interesting problem-solving opportunities for students, performers, and audience members that would not be possible in either physics or dance alone.

This collaboration provides a model for understanding how technology can affect society. First, artists as members of society are directly and indirectly influenced by their past and present societal context as are all people. Some choose to work on "problems" defined in the past, some on those inspired by the newest ideas, materials, products, social concerns, and the like. For the latter group of artists, current technology can provide new aesthetic problems to be mined—the technology both limiting the artist to particular expressions and at the same time opening new possibilities. Dancers performing with the motion detector, for example, must learn complex sets of mental maneuvers which place them in the unusual situation of needing to rely both on their kinesthetic and intellectual powers equally. Such would not be the case with the role of the Sugar Plum Fairy in the "Nutcracker" where physical, kinesthetic, and emotional skills are mostly required. Even in improvisational dance where performers are both creating and performing simultaneously, objective intellectual operations are not necessarily required. So, the motion detector "problem" demands a different balance of skills for the dancer in performance, thus extending the art form in a new direction.

This collaboration also represents a case in which the creative process for both the scientist and choreographer are similar. Although some dance is created from the motivating force of emotion, visual design, or communicating a narrative, some choreographers have adopted a more objective problem-solving approach during the past 25 years. The collaborating choreographer of this project is among those who first conceptualize problems and commit to ideas before generating movement materials and deciding on the exact "flavor" of a dance—an approach more nearly parallel to the objective aspects of science. So this particular choreographer-physicist collaboration provides a working model of the creative process for students while demonstrating how technology can serve as a creative catalyst for choreography. The project extends the medium of dance while dictating a more objective version of the creative process for the choreographer.

Creating a Performance

The motion detector has contributed to major aspects of a prototype performance next discussed by providing a visual display that functioned as part of the scene design. The performance space contained two video projectors with large screens, each of which displayed the output of one of the motion detectors. The movement of two dancers produced simultaneous graphical displays on the screens which created a changing decor for the choreography. For much of the performance, the dancers created the visual display through interacting with the motion detectors which at different times were displaying their position, velocity, or acceleration. During part of the event, the projected motion graphs acted as the choreographic direction for the dancers.

The selection of movement materials and compositional approaches for the performance was influenced by the abilities of the motion detector. For example, when the dancers travel in a particular linear floor pattern, each screen's display is an accurate representation of a single dancer's motion. On the other hand, movement across the detector's fields results in visually complex screen displays that are not easily related to the dancer's motion. As mentioned above, the performance concept also included movement by the dancers, guided by their interpretation of the screen displays. In this section we discuss the various methods by which dancers controlled the visual display and what movement skills and knowledge were acquired by the dancers for the performance. Structural improvisation and choreographed passages were the modes in which the dancers worked. Although sound and costuming are considerations in the performance, only the interaction of the movement with the motion detector and screen displays will be considered in depth in this paper. Another interesting feature of any more fully realized performance will be the role of the computer operators who will act as a costumed ensemble in view of the audience as they "orchestrate" the characteristics of the display for each screen. The dancers, however, always determine the visual form of the graphics by their motion.

The basic interaction of the dancing and the electronics display is structured with the principles of contrast in mind. The list below represents some of the compositional variables the collaborators are studying and some that were included in the prototype choreography.

1. Motion visible by the detector vs. motion that occurs out of range (resulting in "active" screen displays vs. "nonactive" displays);

2. Motion on a linear path in front of one detector vs. motion that occurs throughout the performance space and that intersects many detectors (resulting in "interpretable" graphs vs. random visual design on the screens);

3. Choreography to produce a visual display vs. visual display that controls the choreographic outcome and that produces further visual display;

4. Unison movement of the dancers—one in front of each detector that produces the same display vs. uniform movement that results in different visual displays (each detector measuring a different modality of the motion);

5. Simple harmonic motion of the dancers producing similar position and velocity graphs vs. other motion producing dissimilar position and velocity graphs;

6. Emotionally laden movement contrasting analytical screen displays;

7. Different movement activities producing the same graph vs. the same movement producing different graphs;

8. Simple linear motion producing visually complex graphs;

9. Gross movement with a small scale visual result vs. small movements with large scale graphics;

10. Slow time frame for movement and fast time scale for screen vs. fast time frame for movement and slow time frame for scale.

A discussion of a few examples of these compositional variables may be helpful. Space limitations prevent a discussion of the entire list.

Item #2: Dancers moving on a linear path directly in front of the detector will create a graphic on the screen that may be easy for the audience to connect to the motion. Such "interpretable" graphs can provide structure/limitations for movement improvisation that can be visually simple or complex. On the other hand, dancers who cross in and out of the detector's vision by moving in circular pathways will create a graphic that cannot be easily related to the motion.

Item #3: Choreography can determine the visual display in four ways. The choreographer can predetermine movement design which will result in a choice of (1) arbitrary or (2) intentional visuals on the screen. The dancers can also (3) improvise within the choreographer's guidelines creating the same options, or (4) predetermined graphs can be displayed which the dancers can use as crude notation to limit improvisation. Their improvisations create variations of the original graphics since it is very difficult to exactly duplicate most of them.

Item #6: Dancers can be instructed to perform emotionally laden movement such as wild punches that convey anger. If the graph represented a dancer's position over a relatively long time period with a large distance scale, only the dancer's locomotor motions would be easily visible. Here the frenetic effect of emotional outpouring contrasts with the simple (calm) graphic. Dancers for this performance need to acquire a theoretical understanding of the relationship of the displays for position, velocity, and acceleration to their actual movement. With this knowledge, they can freely design graphics thus acting as both dancer and visual artist simultaneously. They can either have a repertoire of complex designs they have rehearsed, or they can spontaneously design graphs—requiring a most difficult process of the instantaneous transfer of complex mental transformations to human movement. The choreographer can then have the option of creating fixed material or of setting limitations for improvisation as described. The dancers will need to combine a kind of athleticism and wide range of movement abilities with the element of risk-taking in order to improvise effectively within some sections of the choreography.

Conclusion

The end result of the prototype performance, combining technology and dance, created two major juxtapositions for the audience to consider: (1) the special relationship of the dancer and the motion detector as this relationship determined the graphics and (2) the visual aspect of the dancer's movement as it related to the graphics. Although the majority of audience members with traditional expectations can be thwarted if they cannot find narrative "meaning" in these situations, others have opportunities for solving conceptual puzzles, i.e., the exact relationship of the graphic to the movement. With labels on each screen and with the time to observe a variety of situations, a number of audience members actually determined some of the relationships in the prototype event. "Enjoyment" of the event, however, was/will be by no means limited to those who work hard at understanding. Even though the relationship of the motion to the display may not be understandable, the graphics are never random but are bound to the motion by rules. Because the rules are not broken, some members of the audience may internalize the relationships without full understanding, yet gain a predictive capability. Pleasure from the intersection of the visual stimuli and from the surprise of frequent contrast devices are available to all.

The technology in this case is used as a integral part of the performance, during the performance. In the past some choreography has been generated by feeding choreographic variables to a computer which it processes and feeds back to the choreographer. The computer's job is then finished. A unique aspect of this performance is that both the dancers as the artistic agents and a new technology simultaneously create a nonutilitarian experience that has the potential for enjoyment and for the increase of the audience's perceptual abilities.

In summary, the application of the motion detector to dance has required a similar creative process on the part of the physicist and the dance professional. The collaboration has resulted in a specific concept of performance in which dancers have exercised complex mental transformations in order to perform. The motion detector is an essential part of this event with a role that cannot be duplicated through other means. Finally, concepts and processes generated for this performance can be taken into the classroom to create cross-disciplinary teaching innovations in dance.

6 Kahnotation: Computerized Notation for Tap Dance*

Stanley Kahn
Kahn Dance Studio
San Francisco, California

About Kahnotation

Writing about "Kahnotation" is always difficult for me. I never know exactly where to begin. Frequently my notation system is referred to as a "new" way to write "tap dance," but since I've used it for about 50 years, it's hardly new to me. On the other hand, I am still finding

Figure 6.1
Stanley Kahn at the blackboard.

*"Kahnotation©" is the copyrighted name of the notation method developed by Stanley D. Kahn—Reproduction of the system in any form is prohibited without specific authorization.

"new" ways to improve on the application of the basic idea, especially as it applies to the "teaching" of tap dance.

The concept originated in my finding it necessary to precisely express a rhythm as well as a movement. Thus, a sound-sequence as well as a figuration. So, the very first symbols showed the back and forth movement of the leg executing a "shuffle." I realized that the letters of the alphabet express "sounds," and that with only 26 letters, an amazing amount of literature has been preserved over the centuries. Similarly, music notation involving only 12 tones of the tempered scale has allowed composers to "write" millions of melodies, simple and complex, for the inspiration and edification of the world.

It was not without precedent therefore, that I proceeded to develop a system whereby a tap dance might be recorded with rhythmic precision and simplicity. Early on, I found that a certain symbol indicating a particular "move" would have to be "modified" because that particular move could be executed in more than one way, although the sounds produced might be identical. It was necessary therefore to adopt the idea of "exponential modifiers" which is also not unprecedented. Just as figure 3 can be modified by an exponent 3^3 to mean 9, so the symbol for tap $\checkmark$ can be modified by a "heel-beat" symbol O to " $\checkmark^\circ$ " to mean a heel-tap.

Another development was the notion of "combining" single-sound elements to form symbols which expressed as many as five or more sounds in continuity. For instance: the symbol for a "forward brush" is adopted as: " **C** "; therefore a "back-brush" is the reverse: " **Ɔ** ." Combining them produces " **S** ", which becomes the symbol for "shuffle." So now we always hear two sounds when we see " **S** ." It makes no difference that there are many different terms used by teachers worldwide; the sound-move of the tip of the shoe striking the floor in forward motion is represented by " **C** " and in backward motion by " **Ɔ** " and combined they form " **S** " which may be termed a "shuffle," "double," "two-tap," "Shiv," etc. So, the existing terminology may be unfamiliar, but the symbol for the particular movement is the same in any language.

Another point: The sounds are produced by the movement only when the floor is struck; the other foot is struck; or something else (a cane or a chair or a stair-step, etc.) is struck. Therefore, the symbols indicate the striking foot and, because it is most often the "thing" being struck, the floor. When the symbol points to a line on the page, it is actually indicating the floor being struck. For instance: " $\curlyvee$ " is the symbol for "step." In the "Dance Masters of America" terminology, "step" means placing a foot on the floor with a transfer of weight to that foot. So the symbol carries all that information because the " $\curlyvee$ " point touches the "floor" and the "barb" of the arrow is on the right side which always indicates a "change of weight." Thus, "marking time" would appear as a series of "steps" and, as with a musical score, the preparatory position is indicated at the beginning of the notation thus:

Note: In 6/8 Meter, l c 8 is = 4 Measures of Music.

The first space indicates the "meter" of the music; the second space the movements of the feet and which foot executes the first move; the third space will carry information as to stage direction of motion; facings, etc. Now, since "marking time" has no stage motion and remains "in place," no stage direction implies just that! We don't move in any direction, but remain "in place."

As time went by and the usage of k-symbols expanded, I realized that it was an efficient method, and bore some similarity to both language notation and music notation. Both involve "limited alphabets." Only 26 letters and 12 musical tones have allowed authors and composers to preserve eons of literature and music for the inspiration and edification of the

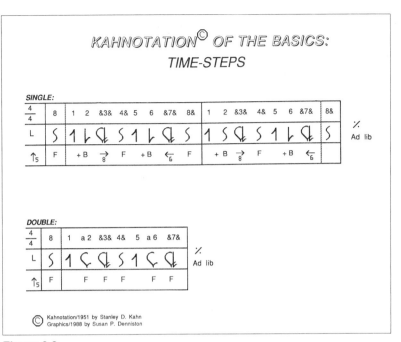

Figure 6.2
Kahnotation of the basics: Time-steps—single, double.

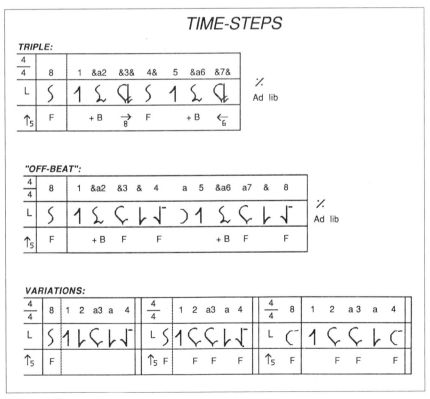

Figure 6.3
Time-steps—triple, off-beat, variations.

world. It is in this spirit that I present "Kahnotation" as a most valuable tool in the preservation and dissemination of exercises and routines in "tap dance." Currently, it is being computerized to facilitate entering, editing, and storage.

Recognition of the method has been certified by inclusion of "Kahnotation" as a subject to be learned by "Teachers in Training." The Dance Masters of America Teachers Training School at Lone Mountain College, San Francisco, included "Kahnotation" in the daily schedule in summer 1982. This is the first recognition by this, the oldest organization of dance teachers in the United States, of any system of notation.

About Stanley Kahn

Figure 6.4
Stanley Kahn.

As a dancer, Stanley Kahn appeared in many local productions in all dance forms, ballet, acrobatic and tap, culminating in a vaudeville engagement with Joe Laurie, Jr. on Loewe and Keith Circuits. As a teacher, he started in 1931 at the Sammy Burns Studio, 1841 Broadway, New York City, and has taught every year since. As a dancer-choreographer and teacher, he was employed at the Kathryn Duffy Theatrical Productions School in Oklahoma City. Later, beginning in 1937 at the Fanchon & Marco Schools of the Theatre in San Francisco and Oakland—and after a stint in the Navy in 2nd World War—he opened the Mason-Kahn Studios at 1125 Market Street in San Francisco. At the same time, he accepted a position on the staff of the Shipstad's and Johnson "Ice Follies," maintaining the studio and the Ice Follies position for 32 years. Kahn is still actively teaching at the same location in San Francisco. As a choreographer, he directed dance, skating, and vocal staging for the Helene Hughes Dancers, the Mason-Kahn Dancers, the Junior League of San Francisco, many of the Jinx Shows for the Bohemian Club of San Francisco, and, until 1982, directed the activities of the Youth of America "on stage." Over all the years of teaching, Kahn has worked on the development of a precise system for annotating dance movement, tap dance in particular. After several years of studio testing, the system has been copyrighted under the name "Kahnotation."

7 A Computerized Procedure for Recording and Analyzing Dance Teacher Mobility

Judith A. Gray
San Francisco State University
San Francisco, California

We have all experienced the loss of interest and attention when required to listen to a teacher who never moves from his or her podium or desk while delivering information to a group of students. Exceptions to this all too frequent phenomenon are the rare charismatic speakers—political and professional leaders, for example—who hold audiences spellbound with sheer oratory and gesture. For the most part, teachers are not trained (nor given examples or role models) in nonverbal teaching behaviors and communication, e.g., locomotion, proxemics, gesture, dramatics, and posture. In fact, teachers tend to make themselves less effective by being, often unwittingly, physically inactive and inaccessible. Inactivity and inaccessibility imply immobility which in turn represents the teacher's lack of conscious mobility behaviors and strategies in the classroom.

The procedure for recording and analyzing dance teacher mobility which follows, assumes that a teacher's mobility pattern constitutes an important dimension of the dance teaching-learning process and further assumes that this dimension is critical to understanding and improving teacher effectiveness.

This paper describes the development and application of a computer-assisted tracking system for recording and analyzing the location patterns of dance teachers. The terms mobility, location, and locomotion will be used interchangeably. The methodology that is presented here was designed to fill the need for precise, objective measures of the teachers' position in space and time. In this investigation, the location behaviors of a teacher were electronically recorded and were transcribed and analyzed by computer. The result is a technically advanced monitoring system which can be used to understand more fully the spontaneous patterns of human mobility in pedagogical settings. This technique is still exploratory in nature and is primarily concerned with describing and examining the phenomena of location rather than with testing hypotheses about the relationship between location behavior and the teaching environment or between teacher mobility and teaching effectiveness.

The teaching of any subject in our schools takes place in an environment which has been designed or adapted to facilitate some range of teacher movement. Teachers display a wide variety of teaching behaviors in response to this environment and, in addition, must negotiate the spatial variables in order to teach effectively. The students may be seated and expected to remain relatively immobile, but the teacher is permitted to roam, pace, withdraw, position, and generally appear more or less active and accessible by means of his or her location behaviors.

Thus it is surprising to discover that there have been few research studies which sought to investigate the locomotory behaviors of teachers. Adams & Biddle (1970) found, while studying social studies and mathematics classes, that a teacher's age affected his or her location behavior. Using a 25 cell matrix they also discovered that teachers spent most of their time at the front of the classroom (70%) with the remaining time divided between walking around the periphery and visiting central cells. A simple nonanalytic tool for recording teacher location exists in physical education for children literature (Barrett, 1977), but it has not been developed as a research procedure. Teacher movements and proxemics have been investigated in studies of nonverbal communication in the classroom (Galloway, 1970) but no method exists to monitor or measure actual pathways. Meanwhile, well-documented location tracking methodologies exist in the areas of animal behavior (Crawley et al., 1982; Stephenson, 1979; Rosenblum, 1979) and infant behavior (Ainsworth & Wittig, 1969).

Description of the Technique

The technique that is presented here attempts to facilitate the observation and measurement of teacher mobility by means of a well-designed computer software system (see Fig. 7.1). It was tested not in traditional classrooms, but in dance classes at the University of Wisconsin-Madison.

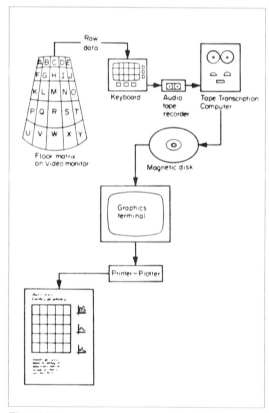

Figure 7.1
Computer hardware system.

Research environment

Since human mobility patterns are measured in space and time, it was first necessary to construct a manageable floor matrix, i.e., one with a sufficient number of cells to generate meaningful location data.

The environment wherein the research behaviors occurred consisted of three spacious dance studios with dimensions of l00′ x 50′. The rooms had wooden floors and high studios. Two studios had mirrors along one wall and bars on three sides. The rooms were lit by natural light. Floor markings in all three studios facilitated the construction of a 5 x 5 matrix for coding and recording purposes. The 25 matrix cells were coded A-Y (see Fig. 7.2)

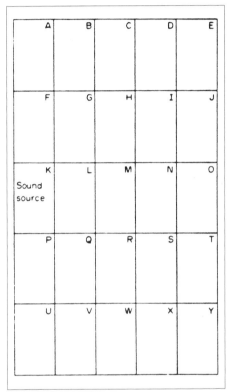

Figure 7.2
Location matrix.

Recording the data

A Sony HVC 2200 video camera equipped with an ultrawide lens attachment was used to record behaviors. It was securely mounted at a height of 10′ from the floor and focused and adjusted to view the floor space. The picture appeared on a Sony Video monitor, Model CVM-960 during actual videotaping. Later, it appeared on an RCA Victor 19″ monitor for larger definition to expedite coding. Betamax video cassette tapes (L-500s) were inserted into a Sony videocassette recorder, SL-2000, which was connected in turn to both monitors. The recorder was equipped with a digital time counter, BetaScan, and variable speed playback options—stop action, slow motion, double speed, frame-by-frame, and reverse. Tape speed was the standard 3-3/4 inches per second. In order to reduce observer contamination, the videocamera was activated by remote control and whenever feasible, was operated by battery pack eliminating obtrusive cables and cord connections.

Encoding the data

A gridded transparency aligned with the floor markings and location matrix was overlayed on the large TV monitor. Location data were encoded in real time using a Sony TCS 310 audiotape recorder for recording keyboard output, a SSR keyboard (Stephenson & Roberts, 1977), a high speed playback tape deck, and a signal conditioning circuit. The SSR system allows for real-time collection of observational data and is computerized.

Observer training

Two observers were trained to record the location behaviors. First they learned to identify the cells of the matrix and memorize the cell codes (letters A-Y). Next they were trained to agree with and abide by a set of observational ground rules, e.g. when the teacher stands on a cell division line, the previous cell will be the cell of record. Finally, the observers were taught the mechanics of entering, by touch-typing, the cell codes onto the SRR keyboard. Trial observations were conducted with nontest videotapes. Since all the cells in the matrix are mutually exclusive, it was only necessary for the observers to identify the onset of a cell change. Thus behaviors could be recorded instantly and precisely and without having to shift the gaze from the monitor or live subject to the keyboard.

Computer transcription

Data were processed by a small computer—PDP-11/20 or Harris Data craft 6024/5. The SSR system includes software for transcription, timing, and organization of the encoded data. These are accomplished by program PLEXYN, a complex syntax analyzer which draws on user-defined values of the coding properties to verify, complete, and uniformly format the entries in the observers record for subsequent statistical programs.

Reliability and objectivity

Intraobserver reliability and interobserver objectivity tests were conducted as follows: Twenty minutes of the test videotape was coded by both observers on separate occasions. One observer recoded the same test tape one week later. Both reliability and objectivity standards were established at or above 0.90 agreement. Once the data were recorded, encoded, transcribed, and Plexynized, pairs of data files were compared in temporal registration by program RLBLTY. This program analyzed the Plexynized data and produced summary statistics from which agreement was calculated. Using Scott's index for code consistency (1955) intraobserver reliability resulted in 0.92 and interobserver objectivity in 0.91.

Validation

Since this study was the first to investigate the phenomenon of teacher location, and no previous theories, scores or results were available, validation of the instrument was limited to determining face-validation and internal construct validation.

Validation issues concerned the following questions:

1. Were the size and number of cells in the matrix sufficiently reasonable for the meaningful measurement of human movement?

2. Was the cell matrix of the floor adequately represented by the facsimile matrix on the video monitor?

Given the size of the dance studios and the absence of nonnegotiable obstacles, it was felt that the 25 cell matrix was logical and adequate for obtaining meaningful distinctions relating to intercell movement by the subjects. Moreover, it was argued that fewer, larger cells would provide logically meaningless data and the same or less location information. It was further hypothesized that a matrix consisting of more cells of smaller dimensions would jeopardize reliability and objectivity and not necessarily provide more meaningful distinctions. This hypothesis proved correct after a 36 cell grid was deployed to record the data. Reliability decreased to 0.86 and objectivity to 0.85. Results of the data analysis showed negligible differences between the 25 and 36 cell matrices.

The accurate replication of the floor matrix on the video-monitor screen was established by comparing a live coding of the location behaviors of a subject with the videotaped version. Floor measurements and distinctive markings were used to reconstruct the matrix grid onto the monitor screen. An intraobserver reliability test resulted in 0.90 percent agreement between the live recorded data and the videotaped recorded data. The instrument thus appeared to be defensible in terms of validity.

Computer graphics and analysis

After data were Plexynized, they were stored on computer disk and magnetic tape. For analysis purposes, it was decided to have multiple indicators of the phenomenon. Location behaviors were quantified in terms of eight measures as follows:

1. Mean incidence per cell = MIN;
2. Mean duration per cell = MDU;
3. Total number of cell changes = TNC;
4. Total number of empty cells = NEC;
5. Total distance travelled = TDT;
6. Mean distance from cell K (source of sound accompaniment) = MDK;
7. Left-right orientation ratio = LRO;
8. Rate of cell change (per minute) = ROC.

In addition, a Versatec electrostatic plotter was employed to graphically represent the actual pathways. Both the location measures and the mobility patterns for each teacher being observed appeared on the video display monitor and then were printed out as hard copy (see Fig. 7.3)

The graphics plotter program was designed to scan the encoded data, apply mathematical and statistical operations, plot the cell changes onto a 25 cell grid, and finally output the completed document. The program was written by Ravi Kochhar and ran on a Harris minicomputer.

Conclusion

The foregoing technique, including data acquisition, data analysis, and a graphic output, represents a superior approach to the analysis of dance teacher locomotion. Permanent storage of behavior using noninvasive video equipment permits unlimited replay of behavioral sequences for verification. The SSR keyboard and accessories allow the user to encode mobility sequences in real time and with a minimum of observer error or interference. The encoded data, in its timed and organized configuration, is compatible for computer input and analysis using a standard statistical analysis package. In short, the system drastically

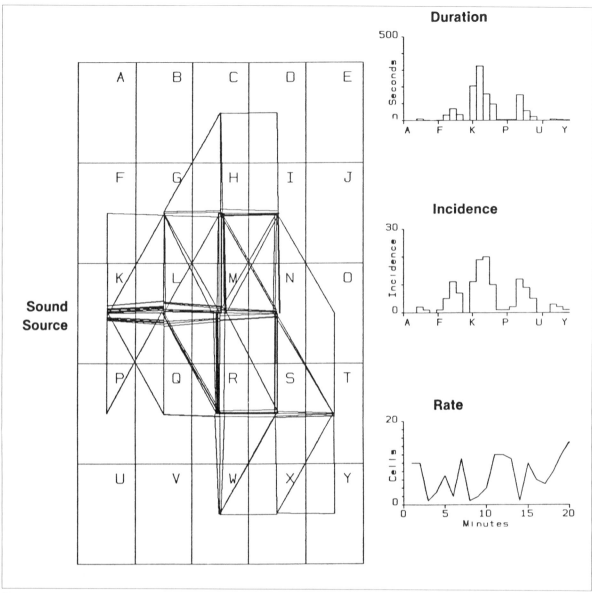

Figure 7.3
Dance teacher location patterns.

reduces the human error factor common to most observational situations; it eliminates the subjective "gut-feeling" approach to behavioral observation analysis and it permits the complex analysis of a large number of variables simply and directly.

Uses

The research suggested that information on observed teaching location behaviors may be an important parameter when describing the variations between and within teacher populations. A correlation analysis could provide both a model and a better perspective from which to evaluate teacher behavior and to make predictions about variations. The study of quantitative aspects of teacher mobility can, I believe, create a vantage point for the study of the entire teaching-learning process.

It is beyond the scope of the present study, but nevertheless well within the capabilities of the procedure, to explore other aspects of location patterns and discuss how they affect this process. Further research should consider the relationship between teacher location and such variables as class size and composition, teaching fatigue, teacher motivation, student and teacher feedback, and teacher behavior variability.

Experimental studies might be designed to determine if certain measures of mobility, rate of cell change for instance, are typical in slow learner situations and if so, are they related to student learning? Other studies might be designed to test whether teacher mobility is related to teacher accessibility, especially in terms of the student's perception of that accessibility. Time-series studies might ascertain whether mobility changes at a specific point in the series and would also determine mobility trends over time, i.e., increase, decrease, or episodal, with or without treatment or intervention. Mobility patterns of teachers could be compared across content area (languages v. mathematics v. music), grade levels, time of day, and size of teaching space. Once it is determined that certain measures of mobility are positively correlated with certain measures of learning, or change, or achievement, then steps could be taken to incorporate these findings in pre-service and in-service dance teacher training. For now, it is clear that a technically advanced methodology exists to track and quantify human location behaviors. This technique can provide opportunities to investigate critical relationships that occur in pedagogical situations and apply them to improving teaching.

Summary

A dance teacher's mobility, and subsequent accessibility, in the dance teaching space can be ascertained by his or her locomotory behaviors. This chapter has described a computer-aided tracking system for recording and analyzing the location patterns of teachers. The procedure presented here will enable researchers to monitor dance teacher mobility and to design correlational and time-series experiments, the results of which could lead to a better understanding of the nonverbal teaching-learning process.

Acknowledgements

This study was made possible, in part, by a grant from the Spencer Foundation to the School of Education, University of Wisconsin-Madison.

Notes

[1] PLEXYN—concept by Gordon R. Stephenson and Daniel P. B. Smith (1968). Original code in SNOBOL IV by Smith from the Univac 1108 computer (1970). Redesigned for testing social interactions between members of a pair of organisms (called PARSYN for pair syntax) and rewritten in FORTRAN IV by Stephenson for the Harris (1976). Expanded by Stephenson into PLEXYN (for complex syntax) to handle the general case (1977). Adapted to Harris under time-sharing mode by Paul S. Tsui and Gordon R. Stephenson (1979). Adapted to PDP-11/23

computer under RT-11 operating system by Nickolas K. Mankovich (1980). Revised by Stephenson to better accommodate a new series of programs specially designed for social interaction analysis (1982).

[2] GKLTS—Gray-Kochhar Location Tracking System. Concept by Judith A. Gray (1982). Written in FORTRAN by Ravi Kochhar (1982) for the Harris 6024/5 minicomputer at the Department of Neurophysiology, University of Wisconsin-Madison and revised to include histograms for illustrating incidence, duration, and rate of cell change (1983).

References

Adams, R. & Biddle, B. (1970). *Realities of teaching: Explorations with videotape.* New York: Holt.

Ainsworth, M & Wittig B. (1969). Attachment and exploratory behavior of one-year olds in a strange situation. In B. M. Foss (Ed.) *Determinants of infant behavior, vol. 4.* London: Methuen.

Barrett, K. (1977). Studying teaching—a means for becoming a more effective teacher. In Logsdon, Barrett, Ammons, Broer, Halverson, Mc Gee, & Roberton (Eds.), *Physical education for children: A focus on the teaching process.* Philadelphia: Lea & Febiger, 271–272.

Crawley, J., Szaras, G., Pryon, C., Creveling, C., & Bernard, B. (1982). Development and evaluation of a computer-automated color T.V. tracking system for automatic recording of the social and exploratory behavior of small animals. *Journal of Neuroscience Methods, 5,* 234–247.

Galloway, C. (1970). Teaching is communicating: Non-verbal language in the classroom. *Association for Student Teaching,* Bulletin No. 29. Washington DC: National Endowment for the Arts.

Rosenblum, L. (1979). Monkeys in time and space. In M. E. Lamb, S. J. Suomi, & G. R. Stephenson (Eds.), *Social interaction analysis.* Madison, WI: University of Wisconsin Press, 269–290.

Scott, W. (1955). Reliability of content analysis: The case for nominal scale coding. *Public Opinion Quarterly,* Fall, 322-325.

Stephenson, G. (1979). PLEXYN: A computer-compatible grammar for coding complex social interactions. In M. E. Lamb, S. J. Suomi, & G. R. Stephenson, *Social interaction analysis.* Madison, WI: University of Wisconsin Press, 157–184.

Stephenson G., & Roberts, T. (1977). The SSR System 7: A general encoding system with computerized transcription. *Behavioral Research Methods and Instrumentation, 9,* 434–441.

8 A Computer Program for the Entry of Benesh Movement Notation

Fred M. Hagist, George Politis
Basser Department of Computer Science
University of Sydney, Australia.

Dancers have had to face the problem of how to record their movements in a way that is economical of time and effort, but that allows accurate reconstruction of the movements. One scheme for recording human movement is Benesh Movement Notation (B.M.N.) (Benesh and Benesh 1977; McGuinnes-Scott). This notation is very adaptable and has been used in fields such as dance, sport, and physiotherapy.

An efficient means of creating, modifying, storing, and retrieving scores of movement notation would be a very valuable tool for anyone who has a serious interest in recording human movement (Brown et al., 1978; Singh et al., 1983). A graphical editor for B.M.N. would hence be an excellent tool for handling scores, as long as the editor is easy to use and efficient in its use of resources.

Editors for another notation, called Labanotation [Hutchinson 1970], have been developed in the past (Brown et al., 1978; Savage & Officer, 1978; Calvert & Chapman, 1978; Sealey, 1980), as well as editors for B.M.N. more recently (Singh et al.,1983; Hughes-Ryman & Ryman, 1985). The motivation for developing a B.M.N. editor here was the need for a means of input to an existing interpreter for the notation (Politis & Herbison-Evans, 1987), that is, a system for taking a score and generating animation of a figure performing the movements specified in the score. Researchers have developed interpreters for Labanotation and have noted the possible applications of a combined editor/interpreter system (Smoliar & Weber,1977; Barenholtz et al., 1977).

This paper describes BED, the editor that was developed for this purpose. The paper will first outline what aspects of Benesh Movement Notation it is currently capable of handling. It will then describe the user interface and capabilities of the editor. The user interface has been carefully designed to try to provide the user with adequate feedback at every step, to have an easy to learn command language, and to have the displayed information organized as ergonomically as possible (Newman & Sproull, 1979).

Benesh Movement Notation

This section gives a brief description of those aspects of B.M.N. that have been implemented in the editor. At the same time, it serves as a brief explanation of the notation for the unfamiliar reader.

The notation is written on a five line music stave. Forming a matrix for the human figure, the lines represent floor level, knee height, shoulder height and top of head (Figure 8.1). Since human height approximately equals arm span, any upright orientation can be drawn in a square called a frame. A sequence of frames representing the body's movement for an entire specific action, such as a dance, is called a score.

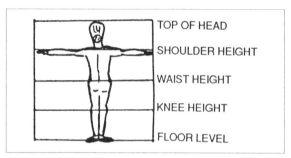

Figure 8.1
Five line stave forming a matrix for the human figure.

Movements and postures are recorded as they would be seen if observed from behind the performer. To record an orientation of the four limbs, it is only necessary to note the positions of both hands and both feet. Each of these parts of the body is notated with a –, |, or •, depending upon whether it is in the plane of the body, in front of the body, or behind it (Figure 8.2). If an arm or a leg is bent, it is also necessary to note the position of the elbow or knee. The signs for an elbow or knee within, in front of, or behind the plane of the body are +, † and ✗ respectively.

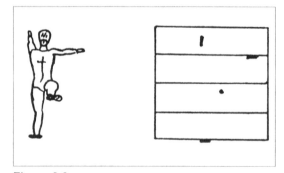

Figure 8.2
The arabesque.

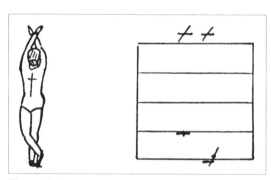

Figure 8.3
A position demonstrating the use of cross-overs.

Since the same sign may represent any of four parts of the body, possible ambiguity is removed as follows. Each limb has its own quadrant of the frame. If ambiguity arises when a body part has moved too far left or right, its sign is crossed with a / sign (Figure 8.3). If ambiguity arises because a body part has moved too high or low, its sign is crossed with a \ sign. To show a hand or foot contacting another part of the body, a small diagonal line is used. A right diagonal slope / means a right hand or foot touching, while a left diagonal slope \ means a left hand or foot touching. If a hand or foot contacts the front of a part of the body, then a dash is added at right angles to the sign. If it contacts behind, then a tiny circle is added. For example, a left foot contacting the front of the body is ⌉ ; a right hand contacting the body from behind is ⌐.

A long dash, —, indicates feet together. The sign for hand together is V. Other signs that

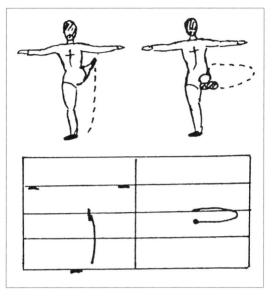

Figure 8.4
Movement lines being used to notate motion.

are implemented but which are too complicated to explain here are •⟶, ⟶•, ⊢, –|, ○⟶, ⟶○ and ○. The notation was invented to record movement, not just stationary positions. When an arm or leg moves, its movement is represented within a frame by tracing the parallel projection of the path of the moving part onto the frame (Figure 8.4). Note that is it not necessary to record any part of the body that has not yet moved, until the next time it does move, or until some ambiguity might arise by its omission. Movements of the head and body can be recorded in B.M.N. but have not yet been implemented in the editor.

Bed: A Benesh Editor

Software and Hardware

BED was written in the C programming language (Kernighan & Ritchie, 1978). It runs on a SUN 2 workstation under the UNIX operating system (Bourne, 1983), and uses the SunCore graphics package (Sun Core, 1984).

The input devices required are a keyboard and a mouse. Once the editor is invoked, the keyboard is only used for entry of file names. All other input is through the mouse. Our mouse has three buttons, though only two are used.

The output device used is a black and white monitor. Although a color device was available, black and white was chosen because it would cause fewer problems were we to port the program to another machine.

Using the editor

The user sits at the workstation and issues an operating system command to begin execution of the editor. An existing score may be edited, or a new score may be created from scratch.

Once the editor has begun executing, the mouse is used to select commands from a menu. Menus make it very difficult to enter incorrect commands, as could be the case with a keyboard-based user interface. All the information needed to use the editor, including all possible commands, is present on the screen.

On the screen is a cursor that follows the movements of the mouse. The cursor is a visual pointer to anything on the screen. When the mouse's left-hand button is depressed, whatever the cursor is pointing to is selected. If the cursor is pointing to a command in a menu, that command is executed. The mouse's right-hand button is used when entering signs and movement lines.

The editor can be thought of as a tool for performing operations on B.M.N. scores. It stores a score as a sequence of frames. For each frame it stores its component signs and movement lines. If the entire score is too big to fit on the screen, only what fits is shown. The rest is stored in computer memory and can be accessed when required.

Displays

The screen can show two possible displays. The first display, which appears when the editor is invoked, shows a menu of commands and the score (Figure 8.5). More correctly, it shows the portion of the score that fits on the screen, a maximum of 36 frames, called the current page. It also shows the cursor, and it has an area reserved for messages from the editor to the user. The first display is used to perform actions that affect the entire score, sections of the score, or entire frames. It cannot be used to affect the contents of any particular frame.

The first display shows a frame with a box around it, called the current frame. It is the frame in the current page that is being considered or acted upon at present. Whenever the user chooses a frame with the mouse and cursor, it becomes the current frame. The concept of the current frame is important because most commands act upon it or in relation to it.

The first display may also show special header and tailer frames. If the first frame of the score is in the current page, the header frame is shown to indicate the beginning of the score. Similarly, if the last frame of the score is currently visible, the tailer frame is drawn on the screen to signify the end of the score.

To insert or alter details in a frame, the user must first make it the current frame, and then issue a command for the second display to be shown. The second display shows a command menu, a menu of signs, the cursor, the current frame enlarged, and has a space reserved for messages (Figure 8.6). The current frame is drawn enlarged by a factor of four so as to allow accurate placing of signs and movement lines.

Commands in the first display. In the first display, most commands fall into five groups, namely, commands that (a) deal with the score, (b) deal with frames, (c) select groups of frames, (d) allow access to the second display, and (e) scroll the screen. There is also a QUIT command, a HELP command, and an ABORT facility.

Score commands. The NAME command causes the current name of the score to appear. Originally, this will be the name of the file from which the score was taken. The command also gives the user the option to type in a new name.

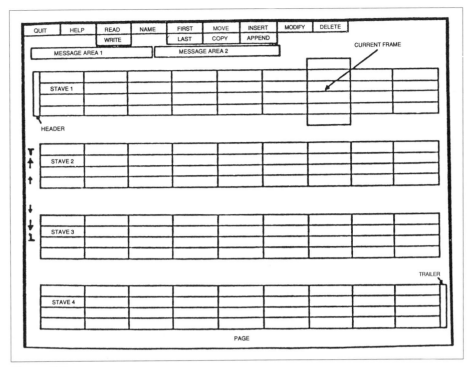

Figure 8.5
The first display.

The WRITE command stores the score as it currently exists onto a file whose name is the current name of the score. The user may also type in an alternate name to be used instead of the current name.

The READ command causes a file, whose name must be typed in, to be read by the editor and be interpreted as Benesh notation. The contents of the file are inserted into the score, either after the current frame, or at the end of the score, according to the user's choice. The READ command would be useful for accessing a library of commonly used movement sequences. These sequences could be entered once, saved on separate files as a library, and inserted into scores as often as required.

Groups of frames. A sequence of frames can be selected as a group for purposes of subsequent moving, copying, or deletion (see below). The FIRST command causes the current frame to become the last frame of the sequence. The purpose of permitting operations on groups of frames is for the user's convenience. The user can, for example, duplicate a dozen frames all at once rather than having to duplicate them one by one.

Frame and group commands. Commands that can be applied to frames or groups of frames are as follows: DELETE will cause the current frame, or the current group of frames, according to the user's choice, to be permanently removed from the score. MOVE will remove the current group of frames from their existing position in the score, and will place them immediately after the current frame. COPY causes the current group to be duplicated and inserted immediately after the current frame.

An advantage of editing by computer over handwriting scores is that when such operations are made, the computer automatically reformats the score. No cutting or pasting is needed to keep a uniform number of frames per line of the score.

In order to allow moving and copying to the beginning of the score, the user is permitted to make the header frame the current frame. However, the editor will not permit the header frame to be deleted, moved, or altered in any way.

Second display. In order to alter the contents of the current frame, the MODIFY command is used. It causes the first display to disappear and the second display to appear showing the current frame enlarged.

To add a new frame into the score, the APPEND command is used. It creates a new, empty frame after the current frame, then makes the new frame the current frame, and then shifts to the second display. The user can now insert the required signs and movement lines into this new frame. The INSERT command is similar, except that it creates a new frame before the original current frame.

Scrolling commands. Since the current page can only fit 36 frames, there is a means of choosing which frames in a long score belong to the current page. We can imagine the score being stored on a scroll, and the current frame being its visible section. There are commands that allow the score to be scrolled, so that previously invisible frames come onto the screen, at the expense of previously visible frames which disappear from the screen. These commands are iconic (pictorial representations) and are located along the left-hand edge of the display (Figure 8.5). The small arrows cause a single line (nine frames) to scroll on from the directions they point to. The large arrows cause an entire page (36 frames) to scroll on. The T-shaped icons cause the file to be "wound" or "rewound" to its very end or beginning.

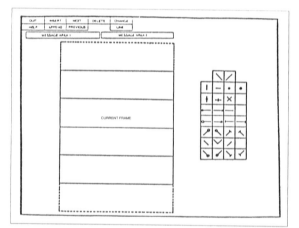

Figure 8.6
The second display.

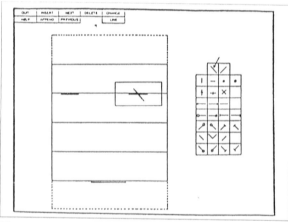

Figure 8.7
Adding a cross-over to a sign.

Other commands and facilities. The HELP command gives a concise explanation of all the commands. There is an ABORT facility that does not appear in the menu, but appears as an option when certain commands are chosen. It gives the user a way of harmlessly changing his or her mind and cancelling an inadvertently chosen action that would cause unwanted alterations to the score. Finally, a QUIT command is used to stop execution of the editor and to return to the operation system.

Commands in the second display. Once a MODIFY, APPEND or INSERT command is issued from the first display, the editor erases the first display and shows the second. The second display shows only the current frame, and has its own command menu, as well as a menu of B.M.N. signs (Figure 8.6).

To enter a sign into the frame, it is selected from the menu. A copy of the sign will then start following the cursor on the screen as it in turn follows the mouse. This process is known as dragging. The user can drag the sign to anywhere in the frame and place it there by clicking the right-hand mouse button. If the wrong sign was selected, another sign can be chosen from the menu. If it has already been clicked in place, the CHANGE command may be used (see below).

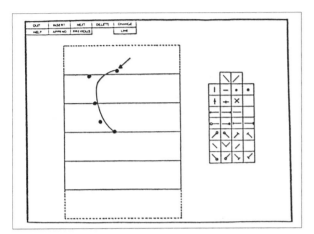

Figure 8.8
Control points for a movement line.

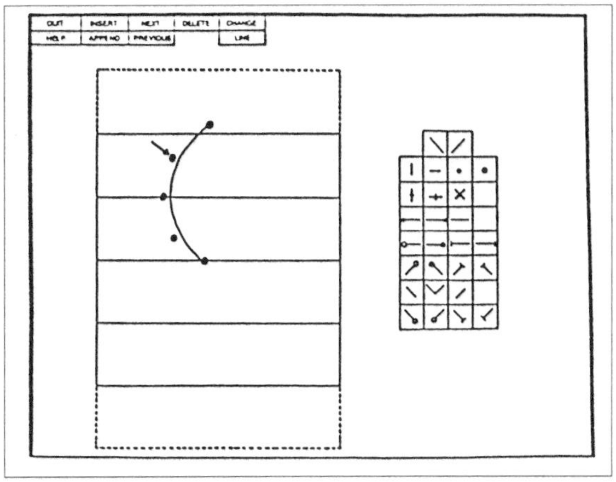

Figure 8.9
Changing control points.

To add a cross-over to a sign, the sign is selected. A box appears around it to indicate its selection. The appropriate cross-over sign can then be selected from the menu (Figure 8.7).

To enter a movement line, the LINE command is selected. The user then must select any five points within the frame with the right-hand button. These are control points of a B-spline that represents the line (Newman & Sproull, 1979, p. 320). After the fifth control point is chosen, the B-spline defined by the five control points appears. The advantages of B-splines over handdrawn curves are that they are smooth and they are easily adjustable. If the shape of the line is unsatisfactory, the user can adjust it by selecting and dragging any of the control points to a new position. This process can be repeated until the line has the required shape. To finish off, the user selects the sign that is to be attached to the movement line (Figures 8.8 to 8.10).

To delete a sign, it must first be selected. Then the DELETE command is selected. To change a sign, it is selected, then the CHANGE command, then the new sign from the menu. To delete a movement line, its sign is selected, then DELETE. Both the line and the sign are removed. At present it is not possible to adjust the position of a sign, nor to adjust or move a movement line after it has been entered. These would be useful future extensions to the editor's capabilities.

There are commands that allow access to adjacent frames and the creation of new frames without having to return to the first display. NEXT causes the frame following the current frame in the score to become the new current frame of the score, and to appear on the screen in the former's place. PREVIOUS similarly makes the frame immediately before the current frame to become the new current frame. APPEND/INSERT behave as they did in the first

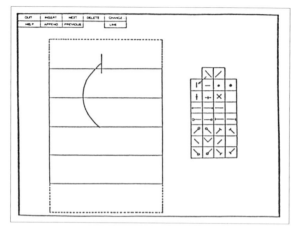

Figure 8.10
Selecting a sign to finish off.

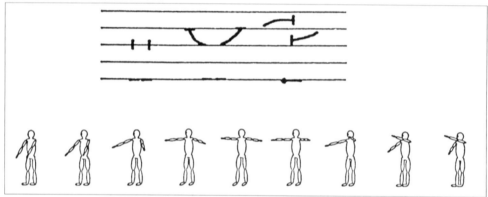

Figure 8.11
A score drawn by a pen plotter, with corresponding BI output.

display: a new, empty frame is created after/before the current frame, and becomes the new current frame.

As with the first display, there is a HELP command, and many commands have an ABORT facility. Finally, QUIT returns to the first display.

Producing Hard-Copies of Scores

Once a score is stored on a file, it is possible to get it automatically drawn on paper. At present, a pen plotter is used, output from which is shown in Figure 8.11. Better quality scores will soon be able to be drawn on a laser printer. Figure 8.11 also shows corresponding output from the B.M.N. interpreter, BI (Politis & Herbison-Evans, 1987).

Conclusion

The graphical editor for B.M.N. described here provides an effective way of entering scores on computer for easy storage, retrieval, and editing. The preparation of dance scores is a tedious process, and a computer can assist the notator in much the same way as a word processor assists in the office.

BED's full potential is realized when used in conjunction with the interpreter. Such a combined system would be useful both to the choreographer and for the teaching of B.M.N., as well as for the production of master scores.

The editor and interpreter have been implemented with possible future extensions in mind. These extensions include implementing a larger subset of the notation, as well as having a richer set of commands in the editor. The system as it stands is a useful starting point for the development of an effective aid to users of Benesh Notation.

References

Barenholtz, J., Wolofsky, Z., Ganapathy, I., Calvert, T., & O'Hara, P. (1977). Computer interpretation of dance notation. In S.Lusignan, & J. S. North, (Eds), *Computing in the Humanities*. Proceedings of the 3rd International Conference on Computing in the Humanities, Waterloo, Canada, 235–240.

Benesh, R. & Benesh, J. (1977). *Reading dance: The birth of choreology*. London: Souvenir Press.

Bourne, S.R. (1983). *The Unix System*. (International Computer Science Series). New York: Addison-Wesley

Calvert, T.W. & Chapman, J. (1978). Notation of movement with computer assistance. *Proceedings of the ACM Annual Conference, 2,* 731–736.

Hagist, F. (1986). *A graphical editor for Benesh Movement Notation*. Unpublished Honours thesis, Basser Department of Computer Science, University of Sydney, Australia.

Hughes-Ryman, R. and Ryman, R.(1985). MacBenesh: A word processor for choreologists. *The Choreologist, 3l,* London: Benesh Institute of Choreology, 25–30.

Kernighan, W. & Ritchie, D. (1978). *The programming language*. New Jersey: Prentice-Hall Englewood Cliffs.

McGuinness-Scott, J. (no date). *Benesh Movement Notation: an introduction to recording clinical data.* , London: Chartered Society of Physiotherapy.

Newman, W & Sproull, R. (1979). *Principles of interactive computer graphics,* (Chapter 28). Tokyo: McGraw-Hill Kogakusha Ltd.

Politis, G. & Herbison-Evans, D. (1987). Computer animation by choreography. *Australian Computer Science Communications, 9*(1), 294–303 (Proceedings of the 10th Australian Computer Science Conference, Geelong).

Savage, G. & Officer, J. (1978). CHOREO: An interactive computer model for dance. *International Journal of Man-Machine Studies, 10,* 1–18.

Sealey, D. (1980). 'NOTATE: Computerized programs for Labanotation. *Journal for the Anthropological Study of Human Movement, 1*(2), 70–74.

Singh, B., Beatty, J., Booth, K., & Ryman, R. (1982). A graphics editor for Benesh Movement Notation. *Computer Graphics, 17*(3), 51–62.

Smoliar, S., & Weber L. (1977). Using the computer for a semantic representation of Labanotation. In S. Lusignan & J. S. North (Eds). *Computing in the Humanities*, Proceedings of the 3rd International Conference on Computing in the Humanities, Waterloo, Canada, 253–261.

SUNCORE. (1984). Programmer's Reference Manual for SunCore. Part no. 800-1115-01. California: Sun Microsystems.

Benesh Movement Notation©, 1955, by Rudolf Benesh.

9 A Computer-Assisted Investigation Into the Effects of Heel Contact in Ballet Allegros

Paula A. Dozzi
Department of Kinesiology, University of Waterloo
Waterloo, Ontario, Canada

The technical demands of a dance performance are not readily evident to the audience. The aesthetic has been the central focus of the art of dance, but the means of achieving this is coming under increased scientific scrutiny. The importance of kinesiology in the dance world has its roots in the classroom where an understanding of the components of movement may facilitate both dance training and performance with a collaboration of the art and science. Specifically, biomechanics provides a valuable tool for the objective qualitative and quantitative assessment of technical movement skills. Explanations of what is really happening in the classroom or on the stage may be found using this tool.

It has only been since the late 1950s that biomechanical measures have been used to investigate the dance world, starting with JoAnna Kneeland's film analysis of dancers in the New York City Ballet, Royal Ballet, and Bolshoi Ballet. Upon critical examination of her films, Kneeland (1966) found that the dancers were performing "in ways which are different, even contradictory to what is taught in the ballet classroom."

Further investigation by Ryman and Ranney (1979) into the skeletal and muscular action in the grand battement devant supported Kneeland's conclusion that classroom teachings at the advanced level are often contradicted by biomechanical principles. In their discussion, it was stated that often teachers' attempts to elicit appropriate responses result in verbal commands which are misleading and counterproductive.

It must not be forgotten, however, that the teachers are aiming for the achievement of illusion upon which the art form is based. From the book of one of the early ballet masters, Carlo Blasis' *A Theoretical Treatise on the Theory and Practice of the Art of Dancing* (1820), it is evident that the illusion is of predominant importance without realistic representation of what is actually occurring in the body. To the present day, the illusion within the art form is still of primary importance as dance teachings, for example heel contact in allegro work, are primarily based upon observation and thus, the aesthetic.

It is clearly evident that the teachings of allegro work demand that the heels be pressed against the ground in both propulsive and landing phases of each jump when done in series. When executing a jump the dancer must press the heels against the floor during the push-off. In addition, the teacher demands that the weight be received by the toes, the balls of the feet, and then the heels when landing. The dancer is constantly reminded of this.

Do skilled dancers adhere to this technical dogma? From observation, it has been noted that often heels do not make contact with the ground in a series of jumps. Some dancers initiate the jump from the ball of the foot rather than the heel (Gans, 1985). In discussions with dancers, many have said that quite often heels do not touch the floor in allegro steps even when the tempo allows sufficient time to do so.

Is the reasoning primarily aesthetic in the teachings or is there a functional, biomechanical advantage to heel contact in allegro of ballet technique? Failure to lower the heels results in the loss of balloon, which is the quality that gives the dancer the appearance of being airborne rather than earthbound, according to Beaumont and Craske (1968). Joyce (1984) reinforces the teachings of toe-ball-heel landings and indicates that not pressing the heels into the floor is a common error in landing. Joyce explained that this articulation is not only for absorbing weight but also for strength and clarity in leg gestures. Robbins (1981) explained further that the heels must come down firmly onto the floor each time the dancer lands—". . . the demi-plié should never be done on the balls of the feet." He stated that this is difficult in a series of jumps at a fast tempo but it means "clean, sharp jumps that are beautiful to watch."

Providing the impetus for the next jump is also believed to be an important function of heel contact in allegro work. Increasing contact area by using the whole foot to push off with is considered to improve elevation.

Although some speculation has been made, scientific research done in the dance world on this topic is rather limited. However, related research has been done in the field of kinesiology and biomechanical applications of this field were essential to this study.

The vertical force-time curve attained from a force platform has been the basis for many vertical jump studies and provides a tracing of the vertical ground reaction forces exerted at all phases of jumping (Hubley, 1981; Hubley & Wells, 1983). The amount of time spent in the air is a direct indication of the amount of elevation and has been the criteria most often used to evaluate performance.

In studies by Hardaker et al., (1985) and Sammarco (1980) on foot and ankle injuries in dancers, it was found that the majority of injuries are chronic and relate to the mechanisms in which the foot and ankle do not properly dissipate repetitive forces.

By registering bone decelerations, accelerometry has been proven to be useful for noninvasive measurements of skeletal transients which result from force transmission and provide an indication of the shock-absorbing capacity of the musculoskeletal system (Voloshin & Wosk, 1980 & 1981; Light et al., 1980).

The measures of elevation and skeletal transients were of primary importance to the investigation of the effects of heel contact in ballet allegro work. In essence, this study was conducted to examine performance from both functional and aesthetic perspectives by comparing biomechanical findings with the teachings of allegro work.

Methodology

Subjects
The subjects for this study were ten ballet students who were working at the advanced level of ballet training. The use of such high calibre dancers reduced discrepancies in the performance of allegro due to factors such as poor technique, lack of experience, and improper body alignment.

Procedure
Sautés in the standard first position were selected since they are representative of the fundamental jumping skill in classical ballet. A jumping sequence consisted of a continuous

series of five sautes aiming for maximal height in each jump. The subjects were instructed to perform the sequence as they would normally (NOR). They were then instructed to jump with forced heel contact (FHC)—pressing their heels firmly on the floor, and without heel contact (FNHC)—allowing their heels to come as close to the ground as possible without touching. These conditions were randomly ordered.

The subjects were asked to perform a practice sequence to become accustomed to the equipment, and were allowed two minute rests between sequences to reduce effects due to fatigue.

Apparatus

A heel switch taped under the heel pad was employed to determine the absence or presence of heel contact with the ground. A triaxial force platform (AMTI-ORG3) was used to obtain the vertical force-time histories. A miniature uniaxial accelerometer (Endevco) externally mounted below the knee (on the tibial tuberosity) and secured with adhesive tape was employed to record the skeletal transients. Data was collected on-line at a sampling

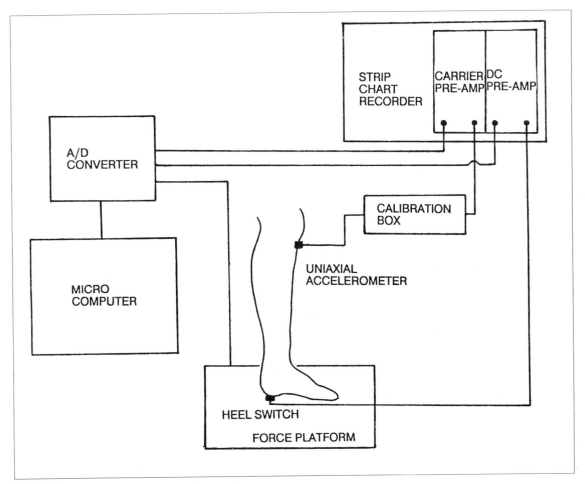

Figure 9.1
Block diagram of experimental set-up

frequency of 300 Hz using an IBM PC computer. (See Figure 9.1 for the block diagram of the equipment used.)

Data Reduction and Analysis

The data obtained from the first and fifth jumps of each five-jump sequence and those which did not show the desired level of the independent variable were disregarded. The subject's results for two jumps in each of the three conditions (NOR, FHC and FNHC) were analyzed. The number of heel strikes, duration of heel contact, peak vertical forces, duration of the airborne phase, and peak skeletal transients were recorded. Elevation, defined as the height of rise of the body's center of gravity, was calculated based on the duration of the airborne phase.

Means of the independent variables were determined in each condition for each subject. Means and standard deviations of elevation, peak vertical forces and peak skeletal transients were then calculated across subjects in each condition.

Results and Discussion

The results are discussed in terms of the questions posed in the study.

Were there differences in the jumps due to variations in heel contact?
Heel contact was analyzed according to the duration of heel contact and the number of heel strikes in each condition. The individual analysis of the condition in which the dancers jumped normally showed that only one of the 20 jumps was performed without heel contact. In her study which was not restricted to advanced dancers, Gans (1985) found that the dancers, especially in the non-shin splint group, rarely contacted the floor with their heels during vertical jumping. Contrary to what was expected, the dancers in this study did have heel contact in the NOR condition.

It was found that the duration of heel contact in the NOR condition was less than that in the FHC condition. There was a greater occurrence of double-heel strikes when the dancers were asked to "press their heels to the floor." Double-heel strikes which are usually attributed to less skilled dancers are frowned upon by most ballet teachers because they give the jump a brittle quality (Gans, 1985). It was obvious that the dancers in this study jumped differently in the FHC condition than when jumping normally. Thus, when comparing the FHC and NOR conditions it is evident that a distinction must be made between the amount of weight borne at the heel.

Did the ground reaction forces differ across the conditions?
The vertical force-time histories in each condition have shown similar patterns for all subjects. Sample heel contact records superimposed over force-time histories are presented in Figure 9.2 and show that the peaks occurred almost exactly when the heels contacted the ground in both the NOR and FHC conditions. The results indicate that the mean peak forces recorded in the FHC condition were larger than those in both the NOR and FNHC conditions; these being 1545 ± 351 N, 1236 ± 470 N, and 1129 ± 367 N, respectively. It should be noted that the peak force in the NHC condition was determined by the first peak which occurred in the tracing as in the other conditions.

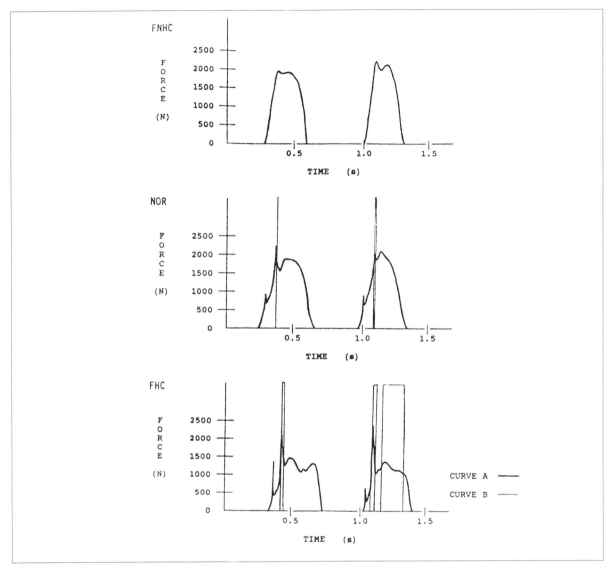

Figure 9.2
Heel contact patterns superimposed on the vertical force-time histories. This figure shows the tracings obtained from two junps by the same subject in each condition. Curve A is the force tracing while Curve B shows the on/off pattern of the heel switch. Note that peak forces occurred at initial heel contact. The FHC condition shows a "double-heel" strike in which the subject placed the heel on the floor during landing, lifted the heel and then put it back down to push off for the next jump.

How was elevation affected by the absence or presence of heel contact?
Since timing greatly affects the maximum height achieved (Laws, 1984), the subjects were instructed to jump as high as possible without stopping. The mean results of their efforts showed that elevation was not affected by the differences in heel contact in the three conditions (Figure 9.3).

   As stated previously, increasing contact area by using the whole foot to push off with is considered to improve elevation. As Karsavina (1968) discussed, ". . . the upward rise is worked in a movement starting from the heel and passing through the sole, the whole

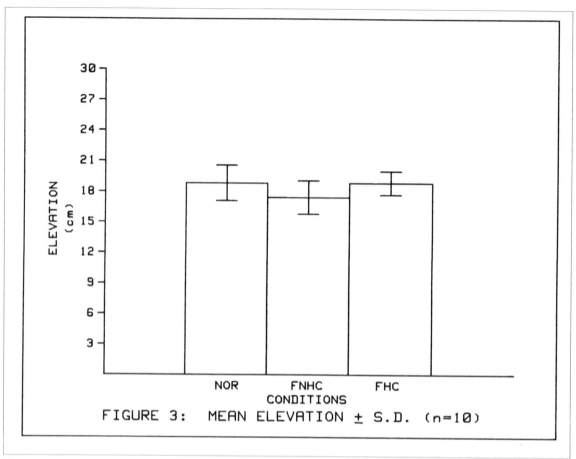

Figure 9.3
Mean elevation.

strength of the foot contributes to elevation." Therefore, it is evident that the results from this study do not support these statements. The mean elevation did not significantly increase when there was an increase in the duration of heel contact in the FHC condition or significantly decrease when there was an absence of heel contact.

What differences were found to suggest changes in shock absorption?
The findings of this study indicate that the shock-absorbing capacity of the system was affected by heel contact during vertical jumping. The peak decelerations, measured as a ratio of the acceleration due to gravity ($g = 9.81$ m/s^2), occurred at heel contact as did the peak forces. Although there were no significant differences between the NOR and FHC conditions with respect to elevation, the mean amplitude of the peak decelerations in the FHC condition was 22.79 ± 2.26 g , approximately four times that of the NOR condition (Figure 9.4). The mean decelerations of 5.81 ± 1.92 g in the NOR condition and 3.76 ± 0.84 g in the NHC condition are reasonable values in comparison to the findings of Light et al. (1980) in his study of artificial shock absorbers on human gait. Tibial decelerations showed peaks of 5 g when hard heels were worn and peaks of 2 g when shock-absorbing footwear was worn, illustrating that larger transients result from inadequate shock-absorbing capacity of the

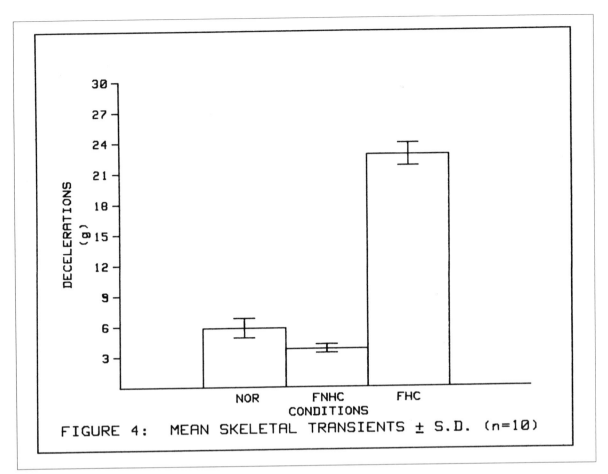

FIGURE 4: MEAN SKELETAL TRANSIENTS ± S.D. (n=10)

Figure 9.4
Mean skeletal transients.

system. The results obtained from this study clearly indicate that more efficient shock absorption occurred in the NOR and FNHC conditions.

These findings show that there is a discrepancy between the instruction to "press the heels firmly" and the maximization of the shock-absorbing capacity of the leg and foot. The maximization of the shock-absorbing capacity of the foot being contingent upon the heels contacting the ground has been suggested as one of the reasons for heel contact in allegro work (Joyce, 1984). When the heels were "pressed firmly" into the floor, the shock-absorbing capacity of the system decreased.

A possible explanation lies in the fact that perhaps the heel must contact lightly, within the constraints of ballet technique, to optimize the shock absorption within the foot. Because the longitudinal arch yields slightly when weight is put on it and recoils when removed (Moore, 1984), light heel contact may maximize the shock-absorbing capacity of the foot and thus, aid in maximizing the attenuation of force waves in the system. When too much weight is placed on the heel, the maximal shock-absorbing capacity of the foot may not be used optimally. It is further suggested that the decelerations incurred during impact may be attenuated by lightly contacting the heels to the floor; during this action the calf muscles remain in tension and thereby, help to dissipate the impact forces. Not pressing the heels firmly into the floor may increase the shock-absorbing capacity of the system.

In accordance with previous studies (Voloshin & Wosk, 1980 and 1981; Light et al., 1980), it has been shown that force wave transmission and shock absorption occur through the musculoskeletal system. Specifically, Voloshin et al. (1981) reported that repetitive loading from heel strikes during gait generates waves of force which are propagated through the skeletal system and attenuated by shock absorbers such as the soft tissues and bones.

Although little evidence exists, epidemiological experiments (Radin et al., 1975; Peyron, 1979) have suggested that skeletal transients are significant factors in the development of degenerative osteoarthritic changes. If this is so, then significant increases in the amplitude of tibial decelerations due to firm heel contact may indeed be linked to the injuries which are associated with repetitive jumps in ballet technique. Therefore, there may be implications for prevention or at least decreases in the occurrence of injuries that are associated with impact. These include talar impingement syndrome with the development of exotoses, stress fractures, achilles tendonitis, plantar faciitis and shin splints for which impact forces and large skeletal transients are thought to be causal factors.

Since it was found that when the dancers jumped normally their heels contacted the floor and yet the skeletal transients were significantly reduced in comparison to the FHC condition, there is evidence that the use of the heel may be important to the mechanisms for dissipating and attenuating force waves. A possible explanation may be that a trained dancer who contacts the floor lightly, conforming to the demands of the ballet aesthetic, may be reducing impact forces, and thus, skeletal decelerations by controlling the landing through the torso, hips, knees, and careful articulation through the foot.

Summary

The results indicate that in vertical jumping these subjects did not adhere to the classroom dictum of "press the heels firmly to the ground" in their allegro work. It was found that this familiar classroom reminder results in responses which may have potential injurious effects to dancers. Beginners are taught to firmly press their heels during vertical jumps in keeping with the aesthetic demands. However, it was found that this teaching is modified, most likely through trial and error, and is not helpful at the advanced level. Perhaps verbal commands given to dancers, such as "touch the heels lightly to the ground", may result in a decreased propagation of force waves through the musculoskeletal system and a maximization of the shock-absorbing capacity of the system; thereby, decreasing the risk of injury.

Acknowledgements

Special thanks to Dr. Richard Wells and Rhonda Ryman for their guidance in this study.

References

Beaumont, C., & Craske, M. (1968) *The theory and practice of allegro in classical ballet.* (5th edition). London: Lowe and Brydone.

Blasis, C. (1968). *Elementary treatise upon the theory and practice of the art of dancing.* (Translation by Mary Stewart Evans). New York: Dover.

Gans, A. (1985). The relationship of heel contact in ascent and descent from jumps to the incidence of shin splints in ballet dancers. *Physical Therapy, 65*(8), 1192–1196.

Hardaker, W., Margello, S., & Goldner, J. (1985). Foot and ankle injuries in theatrical dancers. *Foot and Ankle, 6*(2), 59–69.

Hubley, C. (1981). *An analysis of assumptions underlying vertical jump studies used to examine work augmentation due to prestretch.* Unpublished master's thesis. The University of Waterloo, Ontario, Canada.

Hubley, C., & Wells, R. (1983). Work-energy approach to determine individual joint contributions to vertical jump performance. *European Journal of Applied Physiology, 50,* 247–254.

Joyce, M. (1984). *Dance teaching for children.* California: Mayfield Publishing Company.

Karsavina, T. (1968) *Ballet technique.* New York: Theatre Arts Books.

Kneeland, J. (1966). The dancer prepares. *Dance Magazine*, March, 49–53; April, 57–59; May, 65-66; June, 67–69.

Laws, K. (1984). *The physics of dance.* New York: Schirmer Books Macmillan.

Light, L., McLellan,G., & Klenerman, L. (1980). Skeletal transients on heel strike in normal walking with different footwear. *Journal of Biomechanics, 13,* 477–480.

Moore, K. (1984). *Clinically oriented anatomy.* (2nd edition). Maryland: Williams and Wilkins.

Peyron, J. (1979). Epidemiologic and etiologic approach to osteoarthritis. *Sem. Arth. Rheum, 8,* 288–306.

Radin, E., Paul, I., & Rose, R. (1975). Mechanical factors in the aetiology of osteorthrosis. *Annual of Rhem. Dis., 34* (Suppl.), 132–133.

Robbins, J. (1977). *Classical dance.* London: Newton Abbot.

Ryman, R. & Ranney, D. (1979). A preliminary investigation of skeletal and muscular action in the grand battement devant. *Dance Research Journal, 11,* 1–2.

Sammarco, G. (1980). The foot and ankle in classical ballet and modern dance. In M. H. Jahss (Ed.) *Disorders of the Foot.* Philadelphia: W. B. Saunders Co., 1626–1659.

Voloshin, A. & Wosk, J. (1980, October). *Shock absorption of meniscectomized and painful knees: A comparative in vivo study.* Paper presented at the conference of the Canadian Society of Biomechanics on Human Location, London, Ontario.

Voloshin, A. & Wosk, J. (1981). Influence of artificial shock absorbers on human gait. *Clinical Orthopaedics and Related Research, 160,* 52–56.

10 A Computerized Methodology Using Laban Movement Analysis to Determine Movement Profiles in Dance

Mary A. Brennan, Gordon R. Stephenson,
Mary A. Brehm and Mary C. Deicher
University of Wisconsin-Madison

It is presumed that individuals display habitual movement patterns which characterize their behavior. This is easily seen through the work of skilled impersonators who mimic not only the speech patterns of well known personalities, but their posture, walk, gestures, and facial mannerisms. In dance it is also assumed that over time dancers display habitual movement characteristics when they perform and choreograph. Even an experienced dancer with a wide ranging movement vocabulary will tend to exhibit certain elements more than others. These characteristics might be considered some of components of a person's movement and/or choreographic style.

The purpose of this paper is to present a method of determining a person's movement profile on selected characteristics and to provide sample results. A computerized approach to observing, recording, and analyzing selected movement elements is detailed together with the profile of a single dancer observed in four different solo dance studies.

Method

The data were collected on four short dance studies performed by a female dance major student. One dance (Dance 1) was a three minute solo choreographed by her for a composition class. Two dances, of 45 seconds each [Dance 2 (C1),Dance 3 (C2)], were responses to movement problems given by one of the authors and one study [Dance 4 (I)] was 90 seconds of improvisation performed with one foot maintaining contact with the floor. There was no sound accompaniment for any of the dances. Videotapes of the dance were used for the analysis.

There were several reasons for choosing these dances. First, they were different studies done over a year's time and represented the subject's work in varied problem solving situations. Second, the pieces were short and simple in structure and thus easier to analyze with a new system. And third, each dance was performed in a plain leotard and tights which made it easier to see all the body movement.

The movement elements chosen for observation were derived from a framework of categories that is being developed and tested in stages (Brennan, 1987). The conceptual framework is primarily derived from Laban Movement Analysis, a system for analyzing movement developed from the work of Rudolf Laban (Bartenieff & Lewis,1980). In the testing process each variable is operationally defined and observed on sample videotaped data by two raters to establish a satisfactory percentage of agreement on occurrence. The variables with their code labels and the six categories used in this study are: Body Actions [walk (W), run (R), hop (H), leap (L), jump (J), weight shift (WS), close (CL), lunge (LN), lie (LY), stand (ST), sit (SI), squat (SQ), fall (FL), kneel (KN), turn (P), locomote on other parts (LC)]. Shape [shape flow (SF), arc-like (A), spoke-like (K), carving (C)], Flow Effort [bound (B), free (F)], Weight Effort [strong (N), light (L)], Time Effort [quick (Q), sustained (S)], and Space Effort [direct (D), indirect (I)].

The data collected for the movement profile were processed through the SSR (Signals, Senders, and Receivers) electronic event recording and processing system programs. Each variable has a one or two letter code such as W for walk, SF for shape flow (see above), which is pressed on a computer keyboard to record its occurrence. The videotape of each dance is viewed for the number of times there are categories. For example, one viewing pass is for the effort factor of flow and during that pass the observer presses the appropriate code key for each occurrence of bound or free flow as soon as it is observed. The code is entered with the accuracy of 1/20 of a second. One viewing of each dance was done for each of the above listed categories. For the Body Actions category the tape was viewed in slow-motion to provide more precision in recording the exact moment of change of action.

The viewing and coding of each category creates a separate computer file which is run through PLEXYN, an observation language program which provides a syntax for the entered

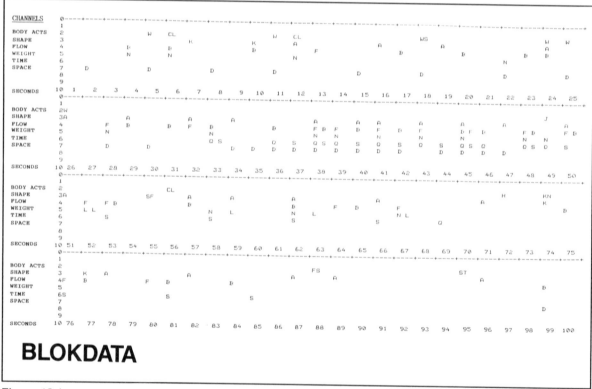

Figure 10.1
100 seconds from Dance 1.

code character strings (Stephenson, 1979). PLEXYN interprets the data in relation to prescribed coding property values and indicates in the output where any errors occur. These data can then be edited to produce an error free file. The program also converts the slow motion data from the Body Actions category into real time so it can be analyzed in comparison with the other categories.

Using the MERGOR program, the six files that were created for each dance were joined to produce one large file which combines all the data into a single time base. This merged file is processed through additional computer programs to provide the next levels of analysis.

The remaining computer programs in the analysis are used in conjunction with dBase III data management software manufactured by Ashton-Tate. This integration of customized programs with established software allows the use of the various dBase commands to manipulate the data into different configurations depending on the emphasis desired. In Figure 10.1 sample output for 100 of the 182 seconds of the BLOKDATA program for Dance 1 is shown. The data code letters are presented horizontally on the page with the number of seconds given at the bottom. Each second is divided into fifths to allow for events at 1/20 of a second. The categories for the data are given at the left. This program arranges all the events that occur each second in a vertical line. Such an arrangement makes the combination of elements at any moment visible.

In Laban Movement Analysis a combination of two effort factors is called a state and a three effort factor combination is known as a drive. The occurrence of four different effort factors is known as a full or complete effort action. In Figure 10.2, seconds 38 to 48 of the BLOKDATA output for Dance 1 is enlarged to show how the effort combinations can be identified. This example shows the presence of the mobile, and awake states, the passion, and vision drives and several instances of complete effort actions.

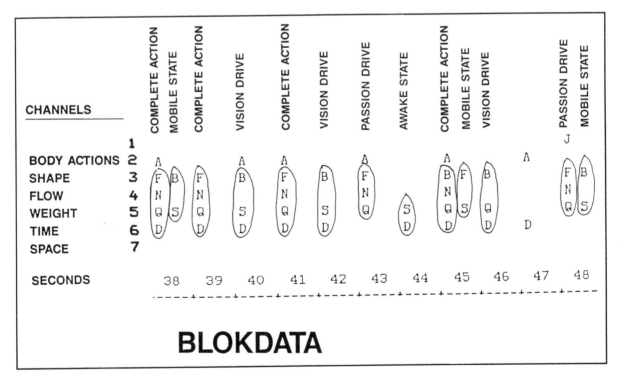

Figure 10.2
10 seconds from Dance 1.

SLICDATA

SECONDS	A	F	B	N	Q	S	D
34	A						D
35							D
36			B		Q		D
37						S	D
38	A	F	B	N	Q	S	D
39		F		N	Q		D
40	A		B			S	D
41	A	F		N	Q		D
42			B			S	D
43	A	F		N	Q		
44						S	D
45	A		B F	N	Q	S	D
46			B		Q		D
47	A						D
48		F	B	N	Q	S	
49	J			N	Q		
50	A	F	B			S	

Figures 10.3
10 seconds from SLICDATA from Dance 1.

ALL PATTERNS

SECONDS		A/CL	B	N	Q	S	D
76			F			S	
39			F	N	Q		D
48			F B	N	Q	S	
16		A					
47		A					D
66		A				S	
59		A	L				
40		A	B			S	D
62		A	B	N		S	
45		A	B F	N	Q	S	D
32		A	F				
43		A	F	N	Q		
41		A	F	N	Q		D
39		A	F B	N	Q	S	D
108		K					
56	CL						
175	CL		F				
12	CL	A		N			
162	CL	K					
49	J			N	Q		
120	KN	A					
117	LN	K		N	S		
121	LY		B				

Figure 10.4
All patterns.

CLUSTERS

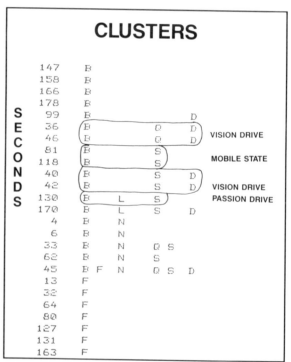

SECONDS	B/F	L	N	Q	S	D	
147	B						
158	B						
166	B						
178	B						
99	B					D	
36	B			Q		D	VISION DRIVE
46	B			Q		D	VISION DRIVE
81	B				S		MOBILE STATE
118	B				S		MOBILE STATE
40	B				S	D	VISION DRIVE
42	B				S	D	PASSION DRIVE
130	B	L			S		PASSION DRIVE
170	B	L			S	D	
4	B		N				
6	B		N				
33	B		N	Q	S		
62	B		N		S		
45	B F		N	Q	S	D	
13	F						
32	F						
64	F						
80	F						
127	F						
131	F						
163	F						

Figure 10.5
Clusters.

Variables and Code	Dance 1 (187 sec)	Dance 2 (45 sec)	Dance 3 (45 sec)	Dance 4 (91 sec)	Total
Shape					
Arc-like (A)	33	12	24	32	101
Spoke-like (K)	13	2	2	2	19
Shape flow (SF)	3	0	2	2	7
Carving (CA)	0	0	0	3	3
Effort					
Bound flow (B)	41	15	25	28	105
Free flow (F)	20	1	7	15	42
Strong weight (N)	18	6	4	6	34
Light Weight (L)	9	3	1	9	22
Quick time (Q)	11	0	2	7	20
Sustained time (S)	25	0	0	17	42
Direct space (D)	30	15	0	4	45
Indirect space (I)	0	0	0	0	0
Body Action					
Walk (W)	5	6	3	10	23
Weight shift (WS)	3	4	5	13	25
Close (CL)	5	1	2	6	14
Kneel (KN)	2	0	0	0	2
Lunge (LN)	4	1	1	0	6
Squat (SQ)	0	1	0	0	1
Turn (P)	2	3	4	13	22
Stand (ST)	2	1	1	0	4
Lie Down (LY)	1	0	0	0	1
Hop (H)	1	1	0	0	2
Jump (J)	1	0	1	0	2
Sit (SI)	0	1	0	0	1
Leap (LP)	0	0	1	0	1

Table 10.1
Totals on all variables for four dances.

In SLICDATA the same data are arranged vertically by seconds (see Figure 10.3). Using this output as a basis and the "set unique on" and the "Index on . . ." commands in dBase III, a listing of all the different element patterns or combinations and the first second where each occurred are given. See sample in Figure 10.4.

By using the "Index on . . ." command with all variables, the total number of all the element combinations are listed in clusters which include all instances of the element or combination. Some of the clusters are identified in the small section of output illustrated in Figure 10.5. In this example there are two instances of the vision drive using bound flow, quick time and direct space and that they occur at seconds 36 and 46. The two occurrences of the mobile state using bound flow and sustained time are found at seconds 81 and 118. At seconds 40 and 42 sustained time is grouped with bound flow and direct space in a vision drive and there is one instance of the passion drive using bound flow, light weight and sustained time.

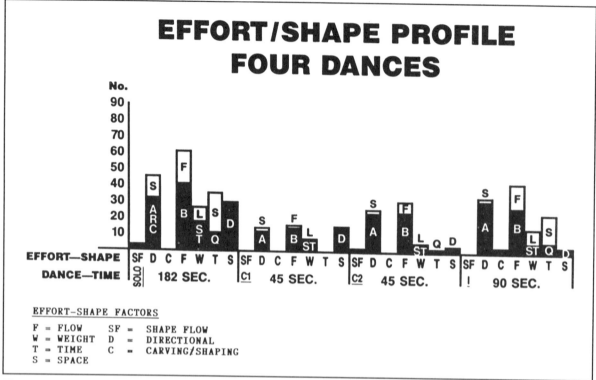

Figure 10.6
Effort/shape profile of four dances.

Results

The SUMARY program gives a total of all the code labels for each merged file. Table 10.1 provides the SUMARY totals for each variable for the four dances. A review of the SUMARY totals shows that bound flow is the predominant effort factor in each dance and for all four dances with a total of 105 occurrences. There is moderate use of direct space (45), free flow (42) and sustained time (42), and less use of strong weight (34), light weight (22) and quick time (20) in considering the totals. There was no observation of indirect space. In the Shape category arc-like movement is prevalent (101). Some use is made of spoke-like movement (19) and little use of shape flow (7) and carving (3). Walking (23), shifting weight (25), and turns (22) are the body actions used most frequently. Other actions occur less often, close (14), stand (4), lunge (6), kneel (2), jump (2), leap (1), lie down (1), sit (1), and squat (1). Figure 10.6 provides a graphic profile of the effort and shape variables for all dances.

By counting the number of occurrences of element combinations, such as the sub-groupings in the effort states and drives in the clustered output, a listing can be made of the combinations. In Table 10.2 the two effort combinations or states are given for all four dances. For each state there are four possible arrangements of the two main effort factors, but not all may have been used in the dance. In the Mobile State, for instance, the dancer used three of the four groupings possible with the flow and time effort factors. A summation of the totals for each combination shows that the mobile state is used most often (12), followed by the dream state (9), rhythm state (6), stable state (5), remote state (5) and awake state (3).

Effort States	Dance 1	Dance 2	Dance 3	Dance 4	Total
Dream State					
free light	2	0	0	2	4
free/strong	0	0	0	1	1
bound/strong	2	0	2	0	4
Rhythm State					
light/sustained	0	0	0	2	2
strong/sustained	2	0	0	0	2
strong/quick	1	0	0	0	1
light/quick	0	0	1	0	1
Stabile State					
Strong/direct	1	2	1	1	5
Awake State					
sustained/direct	2	0	0	1	3
Remote State					
bound/direct	1	3	0	1	5
Mobile State					
free/sustained	3	0	0	2	5
bound/sustained	3	0	0	1	4
bound/quick	0	0	0	3	3

Table 10.2
Effort states.

The same process can be used to determine the type and number of effort drives. The drives which are a combination of three effort factors are shown in Table 10.3. The Passion Drive appears most often with the subject using six of the eight possible combinations over the four dances (total 11). Three combinations of the Vision Drive are seen (total 5) and only one occurrence of the Spell Drive. There are no occurrences of the Action Drive. The subject also displayed five instances of combining four effort factors in complete effort actions. A graphic illustration of the states and drives in all four dances is given in Figure 10.7.

It can be seen from this and the other data that the subject tends to use the same elements and combinations over the four dances. In each dance arc-like Shape movement and bound flow Effort are predominant. This is further exemplified in her use of the dream and mobile states and the passion and vision drives which include the flow effort factor. The major body actions are the walk, weight shift, and turn. Little use is made of other locomotor steps or level changing actions.

Effort Drives	Dance 1	Dance 2	Dance 3	Dance 4	Total
Passion Drive					
free/light/sustain	0	0	0	3	3
bound/strong/quick	1	0	0	1	2
bound/light/sustain	1	0	0	1	2
bound/strong/sustain	1	0	0	0	1
free/strong/quick	2	0	0	0	2
bound/light/quick	0	0	0	1	1
Spell Drive					
free/strong/direct	1	0	0	0	1
Vision Drive					
bound/quick/direct	2	0	0	0	2
bound/sustain/direct	2	0	0	0	2
free/quick/direct	0	0	0	1	1
Complete Effort Actions					
boundflight/sustained/ direct	1	0	0	0	1
free/strong/quick/direct	3	0	0	0	3
bound/strong/quick/direct	1	0	0	0	1

Table 10.3
Effort drives.

There are other ways in which the data from this study can be analyzed and interpreted. This paper was not meant to be exhaustive in analysis. Rather it presents results to demonstrate how a new and sophisticated methodology can be applied to a problem in movement analysis. If only the effort and shape characteristics are considered it can be seen that the subject displays a consistent use of the same variables in four different situations and it says something about her preferences and tendencies in the use of qualitative movement elements. It presents an objective approach to observing, recording and anaylzing selective movement characteristics. A next step and the subject of future research is to carry the analysis into interpretation—to look at the movement as metaphor and meaning.

Acknowledgements

This study was supported in part by a grant from the University of Wisconsin-Madison Graduate Research Committee

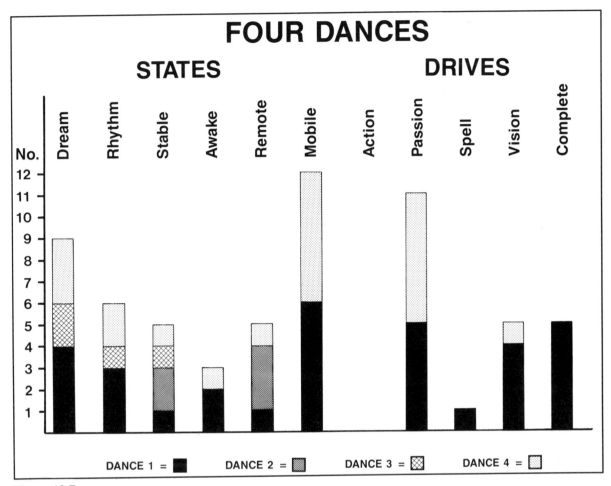

Figure 10.7
Four dances.

References

Bartenieff, I., & Lewis, D. (1980). *Body movement: coping with the environment*. New York: Gordon and Breach Science Publishers.

Brennan, Mary A. (1986). A computerized methodology for recording and analyzing movement qualities. *Dance Notation Journal. 4* (2), 9–15.

Stephenson, G.R., (1979). PLEXYN: a computer-compatible grammer for coding complex social interactions. In M.E. Lamb, S.J. Suomi, and G.R. Stephenson (Eds). *Social Interaction Analysis: Methodological Issues*. Madison, Wisconsin: University of Wisconsin Press, 157–184.

11 The Computerized Production of Educational Material on Benesh Movement Notation*

Rhonda S. Ryman and Robyn Hughes-Ryman
University of Waterloo, Ontario, Canada.

During the fall of 1986, a collaborative project took place between the University of Waterloo Dance Group, Ontario, Canada, and The Benesh Institute, London, England. Six theory lessons on Benesh Movement Notation were produced on the Macintosh personal computer with output from the LaserWriter Printer, using a special application called MacBenesh—an interactive graphics editor for the computerized preparation of Benesh scores which is currently under development at the University of Waterloo Computer Graphics Laboratory.

This represents a major breakthrough in the preparation of updated theoretical information on the constantly evolving Benesh Movement Notation system. Manually produced material takes months, even years, to prepare for distribution to Benesh teachers. Modern technology offers the capability of producing high quality educational material that can be continuously updated in a small fraction of the time.

Background

The MacBenesh program has been under development since 1984 (Hughes-Ryman & Ryman, 1985, Ryman & Hughes-Ryman, 1986). The long-term goal is to produce a program based on the principles of the Benesh system, so that it can be easily used to generate dance notation scores by notators with little or no computer experience.

Benesh Movement Notation is used to record the repertoire of many major ballet companies throughout the world. Conceived by Rudolf and Joan Benesh in 1947, the system is based on the principles of visual perception (Benesh, 1977; McGuinness-Scott, 1983; Brown & Parker, 1984). Frames specifying key body positions are read from left to right along each five-line stave, from the top of the page to the bottom. Musical tempo and rhythm are indicated by signs and text drawn in or above the stave. Transitions between salient positions are indicated visually, through the use of movement lines. Body orientation and travel are also represented as seen, by signs drawn below the stave.

The MacBenesh program comprises menus which organize Benesh signs into easily accessible families, allowing the notator to quickly call up the desired sign or composite sign and accurately position it on the notation stave. An infinite number of movement lines can be interactively created and edited. Signs can easily be deleted or moved. Frames and series of

*Submitted July, 1987.

frames can be cleared, deleted, saved, or moved. Thus editing scores can be done efficiently with considerable savings in manhours. At present, the notator may edit and print a MacBenesh document (a document or file is information created with a computer program) via commercially available applications (an application is basically a computer program that allows the user to create certain types of files) such as MacPaint*, MacDraft*, or MacDraw*. Output is available on the ImageWriter, an inexpensive printer with a resolution of 72 dots per inch, or the more expensive LaserWriter, with a resolution of 300 dots per inch. The former is adequate for drafts, while the latter brings the resolution closer to master score quality required for publication.

Choreologists began experimenting with the program, and soon discovered that excerpts of computerized notation could be electronically "pasted" into text documents. This application was especially suited to producing theoretical material containing notation examples interlaced with verbal explanations. The production of such material has traditionally been done by typing text, estimating the amount of space necessary for the insertion of notation examples, producing the notation by hand, and manually cutting out the examples and pasting them into the appropriate spaces. This process has obvious disadvantages, the most notable being the difficulty in accurately estimating the amount of empty space needed: a single error in judgement might result in the need to retype, recut and repaste several pages. Other problems included shadows on photocopies at points where examples were insufficiently glued, and the extensive recopying required by even small additions or deletions to the content.

The prospect of producing manuscripts which electronically integrated text and notation graphics seemed a natural short-term goal for the MacBenesh editor. Since The Benesh Institute was in the process of revising its Elementary Solo Syllabus (Ballet Application), it was decided to produce selected theory lessons as a pilot project.

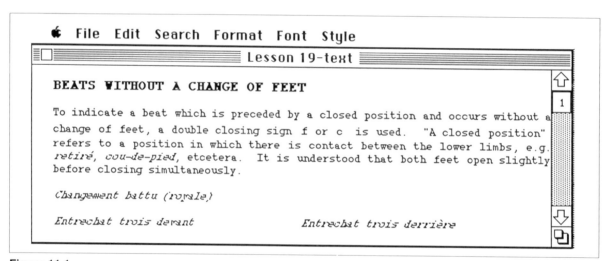

Figure 11.1
MacWrite text of an excerpt from Lesson 19.
* This Figure (a MacPaint picture) illustrates how the initial document looks on the Macintosh screen. Figure 11.5 shows how the final document looks when produced on the LaserWriter printer using its higher graphics capabilities.

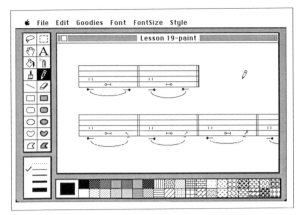

Figure 11.2
Creating notation through MacBenesh.

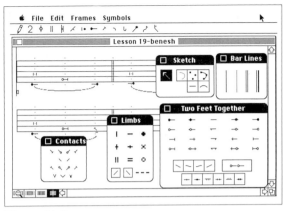

Figure 11.3
Notation saved as a MacPaint file.

Project Description

The Benesh Institute drafted the notation examples and explanatory notes which formed each lesson. Each notation example was produced as a MacBenesh document, refined as a MacPaint document, cut from MacPaint or PaintCutter* (an application which allows more than one screen of graphics to be cut or copied in one piece), and electronically pasted into a text document produced via the MacWrite* word processing application. Both the Teleport MacIntosh desk accessory and the Switcher* application were used to move parts of files between applications. Some charts were produced with the MacDraft graphics application. Some graphics were imbedded within lines of text by creating special Benesh fonts through the Fontastic* application. The final version was printed on the LaserWriter printer. A brief description of this process follows:

Word Processing With Macwrite

First, the text for each lesson was typed and formatted as a MacWrite document. Computer word processors offer a range of options for fonts: typeface (Courier was used in the Course Notes), font size (from 9 point up), styles (e.g. boldface, underline, italics were used for all French terms), and formatting (alignment, justification, spacing). These give the notator great flexibility in creating a layout that is clear and eyecatching.

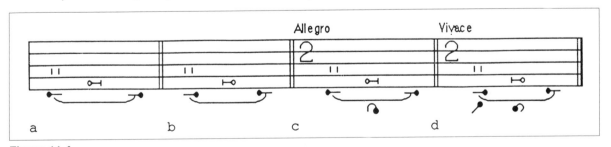

Figure 11.4
Notation modified through MacPaint.

BEATS WITHOUT A CHANGE OF FEET

To indicate a beat which is preceded by a closed position and occurs without a change of feet, a double closing sign ⊢o or o⊣ is used. "A closed position" refers to a position in which there is contact between the lower limbs, e.g. *retiré*, *cou-de-pied*, etcetera. It is understood that both feet open slightly before closing simultaneously.

Changement battu (royale)

Entrechat trois devant

Entrechat trois derrière

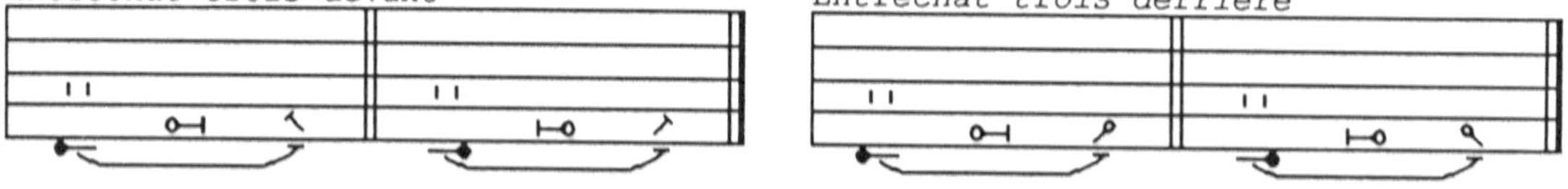

Figure 11.5
Exerpt from Lesson 19: Batterie.

Figure 11.1 illustrates how the initial document looks on the Macintosh screen. Figure 11.5 shows how the final document looks when produced on the LaserWriter printer using its higher graphics capabilities.

To imbed Benesh signs within lines of text, each sign was defined as a Benesh font using the Fontastic application, and installed in the System file. In Figure 11.1, for example, the letter "f" was assigned to the Benesh sign ⊢o , and the letter "c" to the sign o⊣ . The first sentence in Figure 11.1 then looked as follows:

To indicate a beat which is preceded by a closed position and occurs without a change of feet, a double closing sign ⊢o , or o⊣ is used.

Creating Notation With MacBenesh

The notation examples for each lesson were then created as a MacBenesh file. See Figure 11.2. At present, the MacBenesh program accesses about 31,000 Benesh signs. These are the signs most frequently used for ballet classwork, but comprise only about 40 percent of the total number estimated necessary to produce a full range of ballet solo work, including mime and character dance. For a step-by-step description of how to use the program, refer to The MacBenesh Manual (Marcovici & Ryman, 1987).

The notation was then saved in a format which allowed it to be modified, sometimes pixel by pixel (dot by dot), through MacPaint.

Modifying and Transferring Notation Through MacPaint

Finishing touches were added to the notation saved in each MacPaint file. For example, the curved movement lines shown in Figure 11.3 were smoothed and refined as in Figure 11.4.

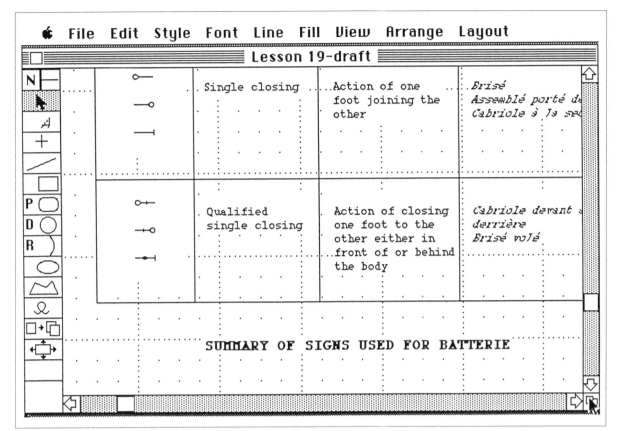

Figure 11.6
Excerpt of a Chart from Lesson 19.

Signs not yet available through MacBenesh, such as turn signs (Figure 11.4.c and 11.4.d are provided as examples), were added, pixel by pixel. Short strings of text, such as musical tempo and quality, were also added at this time. Pieces of notation were then electronically cut or copied from each MacPaint document and pasted into the text document created through MacWrite. The result is illustrated in Figure 11.5.

Creating Charts Through MacDraft

Benesh signs were also created and imbedded into charts produced through the MacDraft application, as shown in Figure 11.6.

Summary

The six theory lessons took approximately 140 hours to create: about four hours per page. See Figure 11.7 for a sample page. These were produced by December 1986, used for a university course from January to March 1987, and updated during May 1987. Unfortunately no statistics are available on the manual production of course notes. It appears that the initial computer production was just as time-consuming as an initial manual production. It is clear, however, that computer updates take less than one-third the time per page as compared to manual updates. This does not take into account possible manual revisions to page numbers and format, should early page changes create the need.

Two factors will favor the continued use of computers for both initial inputting and updates. The user's familiarity with the system will decrease input time to a small extent. To a

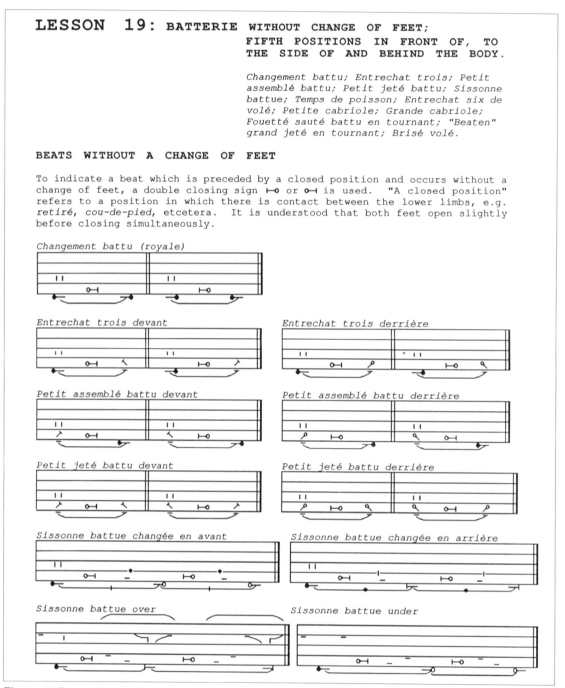

Figure 11.7
A sample page: Lesson 19/1.

greater extent, efficiency will be increased as the MacBenesh program is developed to the point where the time-consuming MacPaint phase is bypassed. The use of more powerful word processing programs, such as Microsoft Word *or ReadySetGo*, will provide greater flexibility in page layout by allowing, for example, the imbedding of graphics directly into strings of text (bypassing the need for Fontastic and perhaps MacDraft). The technology is clearly in place: it is now a matter of time and manpower to actualize its full potential.

Future Directions

The next phase of development for the editor involves the addition of more menus which will access a wider range of Benesh signs. It is also projected to implement the print command in the MacBenesh program, and to store MacBenesh files in such a way that they can be read by the LaserWriter printer, taking full advantage of its high resolution capabilities for producing lines with varying degrees of thickness and smooth curves. These features will allow higher quality notation to be created through MacBenesh and electronically imbedded directly into word processing documents. Bypassing the MacPaint stage will enable the notator to create and edit documents considerably faster and more easily.

In the interim, the editor will continue to be used for a number of projects. Several papers on the theoretical basis of Benesh notation have been produced and are under study by technical committees at The Benesh Institute. Plans are also underway to produce a version of the Dance 341 notes geared to the Cecchetti syllabus: this involves replacing the existing R.A.D. based notation and vocabulary with corresponding Cecchetti examples. Analogous versions are projected for the Russian and perhaps the French "dance d'école." Translations of the English text are also envisioned into foreign languages such as French, German, Italian, and Afrikaans.

Long-term plans for the system may include interactive tutorials available on disk, similar to the CLIP program developed at the University of Iowa (Allen, 1986), and computer animation of notation input to verify and reinforce the student's understanding of theory points (see Calvert,1986; Herbison-Evans, 1986).

The Impact of Desktop Publishing on Dance Notation

The graphic complexity of Benesh notation has long exacerbated the problems in producing publication quality notation necessary for educational material. This has no doubt limited the accessibility of information on the Benesh system. The development of the MacBenesh editor makes it possible to utilize existing systems for desktop publishing to integrate the text and sophisticated graphics needed. This project marks an important breakthrough. The lessons produced are available on disk for revision and expansion, ensuring that up-to-date information is continuously available. It is hoped that this enhanced accessibility will lead to the use of Benesh notation by more members of the dance community, and help dance scripting claim its rightful place in the 20th century.

*Registered Trademark.

References

Allen, J. (1986). Field report: Computerized Labanotation instructional program." *Dance Notation Journal.* 4 (4), 31–33.

Benesh, R. & Benesh, J. (1977.) *Reading dance: The birth of choreology.* London: Souvenir Press.

Brown, A.K. & Parker, M. (1984). *Dance notation for beginners.* London: Dance Books Ltd.

Calvert, T., Lee, C., Ridsdale, G., Hewitt, C., & Tso, V. (1986). The interactive composition of scores for dance. *Dance Notation Journal.* 4 (4), 35–40.

Herbison-Evans, D. & Politis, G. (1986). Computer choreology project at the University of Sydney. *Dance Notation Journal.* 4 (4), 41–46.

Hughes-Ryman, R. & Ryman, R. (1985). MacBenesh: A "Word-Processor" for choreologists. *The Choreologist.* Winter, 25–30.

Hutchinson, A. (1984). *Dance notation, the process of recording movement on paper.* London: Dance Books.

Marcovici, M. & Ryman, R. (1987). *The MacBenesh manual.* Waterloo: University of Waterloo.

McGuinness-Scott, J. (1983). *Movement study and Benesh movement notation.* London: Oxford University Press.

Ryman, R.S. & Hughes-Ryman, R. (1986). The MacBenesh editor: A 'Word Processor' for Benesh notation. *Dance Notation Journal.* 4 (4), 19–26.

Acknowledgements

The production of these theory lessons was funded by the Teaching Resources and Continuing Education Office and The Office of the Dean of Human Kinetics and Leisure Studies, University of Waterloo.

The draft of lessons 15–17, 19 and 20 was produced by Monica Parker, Director, Benesh Institute, London, England. Lesson 18 was produced by Rhonda Ryman, University of Waterloo, Ontario, Canada.

Portions of the MacBenesh program have been funded under a two-year grant from the Social Sciences and Humanities Research Council of Canada, with further support from the National Science and Engineering Research Council, The Ontario Science Centre, Apple Computers, and the University of Waterloo Computer Graphics Laboratory under the supervision of Dr. J.C. Beatty. The authors gratefully acknowledge the work of programmers Doug Moen, Jennifer Hyndman, and Arthur Ryman, and the invaluable input of Adrian Grater, Assistant Director, The Benesh Institute, London, England, who has served as a consultant since 1984.

12 Absolute (0,0,0): Dance Influenced by Technological Environments and Computers

Dianna L. Petty
Brooklyn, New York

The research for this project in computer graphics for choreography began in the fall of 1983, and resulted as part of my choreographic thesis in May 1985. After I compiled a working bibliography for computer and dance research, my curiosity and interest were stirred, and I questioned what research had been done for dance with computers. The next step was to enroll in Engineering 94, an introductory hands-on learning class on how to use a three-dimensional (3-D) Computer-Aided Design (CAD) system taught by Dr. Larry Lichten at UCLA (University of California–Los Angeles).

Technical Detail

The Geometric Design Processor (GDP) is an interactive graphic system for modeling three-dimensional objects, especially mechanical parts and assemblies. [It was developed in the IBM Research Division, and is currently used in the design of large IBM mainframes.] Complex geometric objects are created by generating simple primitive components and then combining these components geometrically. The solid primitive types are cuboid (rectangular block), cylinder, cone, hemisphere, translated polygon (extrusion), and rotated polygon (solid of revolution). All curved surfaces are approximated by planar facets. The geometric description of a single object is called a polyhedron. Various analytic functions can be applied to a polyhedron, such as calculation of physical properties (volume, etc.), and alignment and interference checking.

In addition to solid objects, working planes (2D drawings on a plane located and oriented arbitrarily in 3D space) and linestrings (sets of 3D wires in space) can be generated.

The graphics terminal used was an IBM 3277 Graphics Attachment Display Station, which has an attached Tektronix 614 graphics screen, a joystick and keyboard. It is attached to an IBM 4341, a mainframe computer, on which GDP runs, with a capability of 16 megabytes, or 16 million bytes of storage. There are currently four graphic work stations systems in the University of California, Los Angeles' CAD (Computer-Aided Design) laboratory that support GDP. When I began this project in 1984, GDP was on version 3; it has since been upgraded to version 7 with very useful enhancements.

The project began on GDP as an independent research project, with the objective of designing a technically accurate "graphics dancer." The head was put together from a hemisphere, a cone, and one cone that was flat on both ends for the neck. The eyes were built from hemispheres, and the nose from a polygon (triangle) rotated. A polygon rotated or a polygon translated is created in two steps. First, the programmer must create a solid shape, or a single line image that touches end to end—as if the programmer were designing an image in any shape desired with a single piece of string with the ends touching. Once this initial image is completed, the second step can take place. The programmer then has the choice to either rotate or translate the polygon a certain distance. Partial or whole rotations can create a full circle or semi-revolutions of the polygon. Translations lengthen the flat side of the polygon, creating a thickened, or a tube-like structure.

Multiple copies, like a second eye, could be produced from the first copy, so that the difficulty became positioning the second object in relationship to the first object. This is because, working in 3-D, all positioning or objects must be checked from front, side, and top views. GDP models are built using the standard mathematical axes, known, as X, Y, and Z axes. The user can view the model from any direction desired, in relation to these three-dimensional axes. To look at the model from overhead (for example), the viewer would request to see the image from the +Z angle; to see the right side of the model, the programmer requests to see -X; to see the left side of the model, +X is requested. TORSO faces the -Y direction because the model was centered on the point where X=0, Y=0, and Z=0, or where GDP interprets all its coordinate points to be at absolute (0,0,0). Hence, the choreographic title, "Absolute (0,0,0)."

Building other parts that had softer, more elongated shapes, like the thigh, required the use of the polygon translated or polygon rotated functions. A 2-D outline of the thigh was built using many portions of arcs in order to create a curved polygon that was not completely flat nor completely round. Once the polygon was completed (closed), it was rotated or translated a specified distance or to a specific point. This explains the unsmooth design of the graphic "dancer."

The "body parts" were originally built in separate files for two reasons: 1) to allow for easier manipulation in creating individual body sections and 2) to allow for faster computer response working with smaller models. Files were created for building the head, torso, arms, thigh, calf, foot, hands, and knee. Conscious efforts were made to keep the individual model parts within the same size scale, so that minimal scaling was needed when the pieces were assembled.

Once all the smaller files were moved into the single TORSO file, I was able to manipulate a given file group (such as an arm) without having to move the individual parts contained in the file (such as the fingers). The hierarchical nature of GDP allowed me to move a specified grouping and all its sub-components with one instruction. Individual parts could still be moved if desired, such as the fingers.

GDP's primary method of response is by drawing a line or primitive object per the programmer's specifications. The user asks the computer to move the model, to rotate a part, to rotate a polygon, etc. The programmer can instruct the computer to build primitive objects using specific points or by giving it a general task with approximated points. For example, the programmer can build a hemisphere by either telling the computer absolute position of the hemisphere or by designating approximate points of where the object should be using the joystick crosshairs. The programmer is at a great advantage if he/she can think mathematically, and can estimate what GDP will do before instructing it.

No system of measure is assigned to GDP in order to measure the distance from point to point. Because the system is used as a design tool, it is able to scale a drawing/model to any size desired. It is up to the programmer to assign a system of measurement to his/her design if so desired. I refer to the measurement in terms of units. Small calculations (.0015-1.0 units) were used when detailed movement or parts were needed. Some of the object sizes, for example, were the thigh (.95138 unit width, 1.99 units length), head (2.13007 units length, 1.5 units width), eye (.15 unit width, .25 unit length). Movements and/or calculations can be done from one point to another or by moving from three absolute coordinates which designate the exact mathematical values for X, Y, and Z directional axes. Working with absolute coordinates helps speed up calculation time and determine specific points while building a part to be duplicated. Using absolute coordinates helped when it was necessary to construct models rapidly (GDP can only retrieve and store completed model parts, not portions of models).

Proportioning body parts requires the use of Rotate and Scale function, a percentile calculation used in reducing or increasing the size of a designated model part. Again, all axes must be taken into consideration because proportioning can only be done in one direction at a time.

Creating the first static "dance pose" was more difficult than proportioning the model's parts. Since the pieces of the model are unassembled, all pieces needed to be moved and placed in relation to all other parts—and viewed from all axial directions. Although a specified dance pose may appear accurate from a -Y perspective, a view from +Z's angle may show a part that had separated from the rest of the model.

By using GDP's updated function called Attribute, a model part could be built to designate "joints." With the aid of Attribute, model parts could be hinged at the joint, and could be limited to move in a particular direction, with minimum and maximum points or rotation. This would allow TORSO's arms, legs, and other jointed parts to rotate a specific distance, creating simulated flexion and extension approximated to human capability. This computer function would save a great deal of time in manipulating TORSO into various dance poses, and would eliminate the need to constantly check the model's three-dimensional positioning.

Technical Results:

It took approximately 10 to 12 weeks to build and create an aesthetically acceptable wire-framed "dancer." GDP's limitations were challenging, but its limited modeling capabilities were all the more encouraging to build a larger, more detailed model. TORSO still looks like a robot, but the design became a dancer made from a cluster of blocks, similar to what an artist might sketch if they were working with cubism. The model was very limited in how it could be put together, but by using the polygon translated, polygon rotated, and merge functions, the bulky, primitive structures began to take on the form desired—an acceptable, aesthetically designed "robot-dancer."

Technical Difficulties:

The model exceeded 50 percent of the file's storage space, over 3 Megabytes in size—an amount that taxed 60 percent of the total file space and over 40 percent of what the computer mainframe's memory could handle at any one time. The amount was almost five times the normal student storage capacity allotment—and comparable to what storage the CAD/CAM laboratory research assistants had been assigned.

Since GDP builds polyhedral models, the size of the model is not determined by its size in terms of scale, but rather how many mathematical calculations are required to rebuild the model. In order to create a smoother, curved surface, more facets are required—thereby increasing the number of calculations needed to build the polygon rotated, and subsequently increasing the size of the model. TORSO's immense size did not permit me to view the model in Hidden Line option—a method of looking at the model as if it were to be built in solid form.

The excess size of the model almost caused the loss of the entire program. I managed to purge TORSO from the system, with little chance of retrieving it. After the laboratory teaching assistants' called IBM Systems engineers in Los Angeles, and spent 3 hours of intensive work (trying to reassign the number needed to retrieve the model's spool of information), they managed to save TORSO.

Photographic Detail

Once the model was finished, the next step was to take photographs. Due to light reflections from outside windows, light from other monitors and other people working in the CAD (computer aided design) laboratory, most of the pictures were taken at night. The camera used was a 35mm Canon A-1, with a Solagar macrofocus lens, zoom of 28mm-80mm (our photos were taken at 45mm length), shot at approximately 12 inches from the computer monitor. The film used was Fuji ASA 200, with most pictures taken at either 15 second or 30 second time exposures. The graphics model was then sized to .5 unit scale for multiple images put into one slide frame, .75 unit and 1.0 unit for single images on a slide, and 10.0 unit scale for close-up views of "body" sections.

Putting TORSO into different poses could take anywhere from 30 minutes to 3 hours to take apart and reassemble the model, depending on the difficulty or type of change, and remembering to position the model in all three directions. There were approximately 10 terminals connected to the IBM system, and invariably, working on TORSO would considerably slow down anyone else if they were working on GDP.

Once a new dance position had been established, the model could be drawn at various angles, giving the photographer approximately 4 to 7 different camera shots.

Choreography

The live dancers were designed to be parts of the "machine," or the total working environment. No single dancer is stronger than any other—they are all equal. The aura is enhanced by the costumes, covering the dancers from head to foot; all that is seen are their eyes, hands, and feet. This was in order to remove as many of the human elements as was visually possible. In addition, the unitards are painted simulating the prominent lines seen in TORSO, such as the outlines of the legs, arms, torsos, and the "X" on the head and center of the spine.

A series of TORSO's dance positions are projected behind the dancers as they move throughout the dance. The graphics image presents a pose, which the dancers also do, but then develop into variations derived from the initial pose. As the dancers run intermittently across the stage, the slides change in 1 second or 4 second intervals, showing either the exact poses as the dancers, or faded in, close up detail of TORSO.

The choreography had very little influence on the developed design of the "graphic dancer"; however, TORSO directly influenced how the dancers perceived their own movement and pose interpretations. The dancers observed TORSO's "anatomical positioning," then would analyze their own from all angles. Many hours were spent attempting to make sure the surface of the hands, fingers, and wrists maintained the same flat planes as TORSO had. The visual aid and precise positioning of TORSO made the dancers strive to not only be anatomically correct in their own bodies, but required them to be as near-perfect to one another as they were to the "graphics dancer."

Choreographic/Technical Integration

"Absolute (0,0,0)" began as an effort to design and develop movement on a computer before trying it on live dancers. It was interesting to realize what could be done for a choreographic work with computer graphics designs as thematic material. What choreographic developments could be problem solved on a computer before putting it on live dancers? What possibilities of blending computer graphics and live dancers and been explored? How would computer graphics be received by an audience in an artistic performance? Could it be presented aesthetically? Had this been done before?

To my knowledge, this type of computer graphics had not been used in a live performance, and not in the manner proposed. The intention was to present the dancers as mechanical as humanly possible—at the same time, present a "graphic dancer" as aesthetic and humanistic as GDP could design—creating an intriguing, yet mystifying blend between choreography and computer graphics. The attempt was to create an ambiguous, technological environment giving equal emphasis to human beings and technology.

Conclusion

The overall effort of developing a choreographic work with the aid of 3-D computer graphics took five months, but was well worth the experience. It would not have been able to take place without the support and encouragement from two extremely opposite schools of thought. To anyone in an educational setting, there is an enormous wealth of information available for students, and faculty with increased interdepartmental work. The benefits are outstanding, and I cannot encourage it enough.

Acknowledgements

An enormous amount of gratitude is due to the UCLA Computer Aided Design Laboratory, the UCLA Dance Department, to all those who helped in the various stages of this project. My gratitude, many thanks, and appreciation go to Professor Doris Einstein Siegel, Professor Larry Lichten, Carollee Dunson Courtney, Sam Jones, my UCLA Computer Engineer laboratory teaching assistants (Dave, Marcel, Nader), and my dancers (Anne Goodman, Kim Borgaro-Jeskie, Debra Nelson and Maria Elena Velez). Thank you to Mr. Franklin Gracer for his interview and his comments (T.J. Watson Research Center, IBM, Yorktown Heights, NY, interview, 11/8/88).

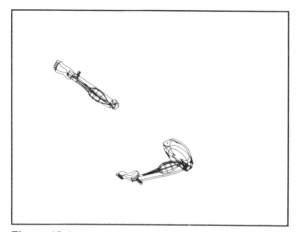

Figure 12.1
Wire-frame body parts (leg).

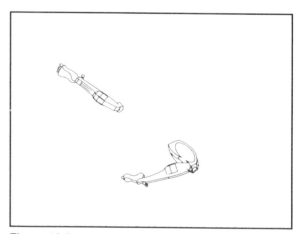

Figure 12.2
Wire-frame body parts (leg).

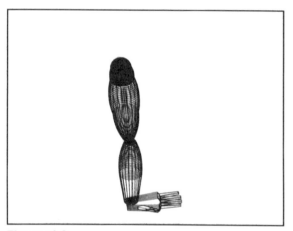

Figure 12.3
Wire-frame body parts (leg).

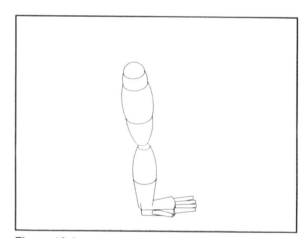

Figure 12.4
Wire-frame body parts (leg).

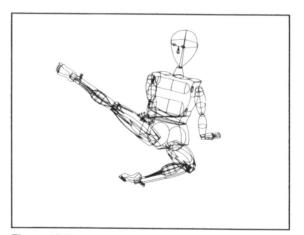

Figure 12.5
Wire-frame body.

Notes

"ABSOLUTE (0,0,0)"	Premiered at UCLA Master's Thesis Concert, UCLA Dance Department, May 3–5, 1985*.
Choreography:	Dianna L. Petty
Dancers:	Anne Goodman, Kim Borgaro-Jeske, Debra Nelson, Maria Elena Velez
Music:	Tony Jones
Costume Concept:	Dianna L. Petty, Stephanie Schoelzel
Costume Contruction:	Stephanie Schoelzel
Computer Graphics:	Dianna L. Petty
Computer Photography:	Douglas Roth
Choreographic Photography:	Steve Lopez
Lighting Design:	Kenneth Lennon
Technical Director:	Sam Jones
Video:	Arsenio Apillanes

*Funded in part by the UCLA Dance Department and the UCLA Engineering Department.

References

Gracer, T. (1984). *Franklin, GDP Primer-Release 3*. Yorktown Heights, New York: Watson Research Center, 1.

13 Capturing and Processing Dance Images With Computers

Judith A. Gray
San Francisco State University
San Francisco

Unlike spatially static forms and two-dimensional shapes, images of the human form in motion can be arrested and manipulated electronically to produce a unique kinetic art form. This chapter describes a system for capturing, processing, and displaying video and photographic images of dancers and includes the possible uses of the system for dancers, choreographers, technicians and teachers. It concludes with implications for the perception of dance and raises questions about the effects of digital processing on the visual aesthetic quality of dance imagery.

Introduction

Although computerized image processing has been utilized since the early 1960s, its costs have been prohibitive. Today, however, several low-cost computers (MacIntosh, IBM, and Mindset, for example) are capable of fulfilling the conventions of this sophisticated electronic process. The capturing and computer manipulation of photographic and videographic images involves a fairly standard digitizing process, an explanation of which follows:

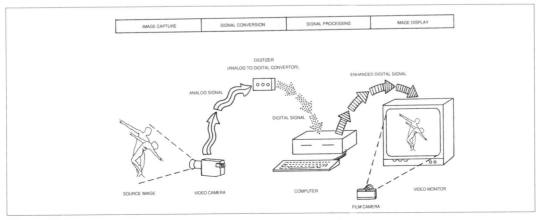

Figure 13.1
Digital image processing.

Digital Processing

In order for a photographic image of a dance or dancer to be digitized it must first be converted from its analog form to a digital one. That is, the photographed lines, contrasts, colors, textures, and shadings must be changed into numerical form—in this case, the binary system. An image that has been transformed into a set of binary numbers can be stored indefinitely in the computer. More importantly, the image can be recalled in its original form or it can undergo innumerable alterations by simply making changes in the digital values.

A device called a photomultiplier systematically samples the light transmitted through a transparent image; a photographic slide, for instance, and divides it into discrete picture elements (pixels), each of which registers a certain amount of brightness. Brightness is a continuous variable and is, therefore, an analog signal. It must be quantified before the computer can make sense of it. A quantizer accomplishes this task by regrouping the brightness signals into levels of gray. Each level receives a number. A gray scale that has only two levels is represented by pixels that are either black or white. On the other hand, a gray scale with 32 levels has pixels that can be black or white or 30 variations of gray. The larger the gray scale, the higher the resolution of the image for display purposes and the more detailed and realistic its reproduction.

Once the computer has processed the digital signal, it can in turn modulate the light source to produce a new or different photographic image by exposing the film one pixel at a time. In other words, the process can be operated in reverse.

Procedure

The imaging procedure consists of three distinct phases—capturing, processing, and displaying.

Capturing
Capturing techniques are either "image scanning," whereby analog images are digitized and subsequently stored by the computer, or "frame grabbing," a method by which a video image is arrested, accepted, and readied for digitizing. Input sources for frame grabbers can be closed circuit, broadcast, or recorded videotaping and also low-light operations.

Processing
The digitized images are processed by the application of a variety of specially designed and experimental software. These programs are equipped to analyze, reduce, massage, enhance, color wash, expand, and otherwise manipulate the input. In addition, computer-generated text, graphics, music, and narration can be integrated or superimposed during the processing phase.

Displaying
In the display phase, the system allows for presentation of the processed images on a variety of output devices. These can include monitors, screens, and cycloramas while freeze-frame and photographic images can be displayed as hard copy by printers and plotters. Modems can be used to display the output over long distances.

Possible Uses

Future development of this technology may result in an unforeseen variety of artistic and scientific applications.

1. A dance could be completely simulated without live dancers. The computer would generate not only choreographic instructions to the dancers, but determine the blocking, lighting, and special effects.

2. Patterns of light and spatial boundaries could be made to oscillate or move around the dancer.

3. Rear screen video projections could result in the dancer appearing to be surrounded by his or her own image or images of other dancers.

4. Holographic dance environments.

5. Choreographics incorporating computer-generated theatrical, kinetic, and sensory effects.

6. A prototype dance could be digitized and stored as a working model to be used to control the generation of further dances all bearing the distinctive stamp of the original choreographer.

7. Laser videodiscs capable of storing all the repertoires of major and minor dance companies.

The relationship between the dancer and his or her environment will be limited only by the imagination of the choreographer and the power of the computer. The prima ballerina of the future may not be a live human being at all, but a digitized visual image with a 3-dimensionality capable of amazing feats and dazzling human likeness.

Figure 13.2
Analog input.

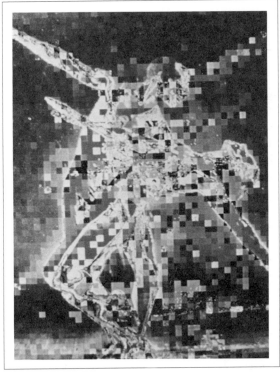

Figure 13.3
Digitized output.

Conclusion

The effects of digital processing on the visual quality of dance images is technically and artistically intriguing. Experiments have shown that the integration of dance and computer technology will change the face and perception of dance as an art form. The system described in this paper has produced the greatest venture into "artificial reality" that the field of dance has ever known. Combined with latest information processing theories, this computer-aided process for expressing and communicating the art of dance promises to impose a major landmark in the history of dance.

References

Badler, N., & Smoliar, S. (1979). Digital representations of human movement. *Computing Surveys* 11.(1), 19–38.

Brand, S., Kelly, K., & Kinney, J. (1985). Digital retouching: The end of photography as evidence of anything. *Whole Earth Review*. Sausalito, CA, 42–49.

Cannon, T., & Hunt, B. (1981). Image processing by computer. *Scientific American.*, 245:(20), 214–225.

Gray, J. (1984) Dance in computer technology. *Interchange.*, 15(4), 15–25.

Krueger, M. (1983). *Artificial Reality*. Menlo Park, CA: Addison-Wesley Publishing Company.

Wilson, A. (1985). Image processing with personal computers. *Electronic Imaging,* 4(3), 44–51.

14 Computerized Lighting Design for Dance: An Interview with David Elliot

Judith A. Gray
San Francisco State University
San Francisco, California

Computer-controlled lighting systems have taken a long time to become available to dancers, choreographers and dance production crews. There are two reasons for this delay. First, the dance artists themselves have resisted the relentless advances of computer technology for understandable reasons—to dance is human, to operate machines is inhuman. Second, the owners and managers of the theaters where dance is performed continue to operate expensive, cumbersome light boards because they have neither the funds, the technicians, nor the incentive to change to smaller, more efficient computerized systems. Furthermore, businesses who lease the costly equipment to theaters and dance companies make considerable profits from their bulky analog equipment. Meanwhile, compromises are made. A relatively inexpensive personal computer is often used to handle some of the standard lighting tasks such as cues for house lights, footlights, and the cyclorama. In addition, computers can store production lighting records and inventories. Electricians and stage crews however, continue to manually operate the spotlights, overheads, and colored filters. The role of the lighting designer, on the other hand, has changed over the years due to the increasing influence of computer technology. Many of them have witnessed the art and craft of stage lighting evolve from cue sheets to keyboards. David K. H. Elliot, lighting designer for the San Francisco Ballet Company, is a case in point. He welcomed the opportunity to discuss the practicalities, costs, and issues of today's computer-generated lighting systems for dance.

1. *How did you personally get involved in this field?*   I got involved in the field by walking in the stage door of the Union Theater in Madison, Wisconsin in mid-September of 1965 to go to a seminar on stage lighting led by Jerry Lewis, a graduate student, under the auspices of the Wisconsin Players. I was hooked.

2. *What are the essential components of a state-of-the-art computer-controlled light board?*   There are four essential components of a computer lighting system: the control board, the dimmer racks, a printer, and a monitor for the design table. A typewriter keyboard will soon be essential as well, if it isn't already. The essential functions of a computer light board are to make control channel assignments, record the levels and time information of each light cue, view that information, modify it, play it back, and print it. Beyond these functions, there are an increasing number of additional features being made available. There are submasters, multiple timed faders, labeling functions, special effects, greater storage capacity, and so

forth. This is a trend that will continue as hardware evolves and lighting control shifts increasingly over to a software based approach.

3. Electronic control systems for stage lighting have been in development since World War II. Why have they suddenly become so sophisticated and prominent in this decade? Electronic theater equipment has recently become sophisticated and prominent because the sophisticated parts are inexpensive (by and large) and readily available (mostly). Historically, the theater is quick in adapting to the current technology, throwing out the old and trying the new once it's in over-the-counter circulation. About the time the first transistors were being installed in radios, a few years after World War Two, they began coming into theaters in tape decks and dimmers. The first uses of electronics in the theater appeared in the late forties at Yale University, thanks to George Izenour. Then came "chips" and the first computer control boards which arrived in theaters in the early seventies, the same time as chips began to appear in everything else—about five years into the Apollo Program. Today it's microprocessors, which not only control stage lights, but also washing machines, automobile engines, compact disk players, and so on.

4. What are the major differences between an old dimmer board and the new computerized control board? The first thing to notice is that a computer light board and its electronic dimmers are a lot smaller and lighter than any of their counterparts. Then there's the number of dimmers. Twenty years ago 400 dimmers would have been considered a large, permanent installation. Today, large touring companies often carry at least that many dimmers, while permanent installations consist of 1,500 dimmers and more. Next, computer-based electronic dimming systems cost less to run. They take fewer people to operate, although there is a bit of a trade off here. The technical expertise level required of those directly involved with the care and feeding of the light board goes up a notch or two. While their numbers are fewer, trained and experienced technicians are essential. As in any profession, the more experienced you are, the more worth you have.

5. How affordable is one? There are ways computer boards can affect operating costs. There is potential to reduce the amount of expensive stage time used in lighting a production by reducing the number of technical hours and/or substantially increasing what gets accomplished within the stage time you already use. For example, time is spent looking at cues, not waiting for them to be reset. The actual cost of the computer equipment varies . The entry level today for the control board component of a lighting system is around $3,000. It increases to $25,000+ to operate the lighting system of a major opera house. In addition to the cost of the control board there is the cost of the other components and of the installation. Which control and operating elements to opt for in a specific situation is a complex decision, given the styles and needs of the performances, the nature of the production period and the amount of money available. Seeking the advice of those who design these boards is a good idea. An experienced consultant is well worth the money.

6. What are the advantages to dance companies of leasing one as opposed to owning one? Your consultant may recommend leasing. The major advantages of leasing are service and repair. Should your board "go down," and it may, a single phone call results in the delivery of a duplicate light board, quickly. The American Ballet Theater, playing in LA, received a board from Bash Lighting in New Jersey less than 12 hours after making a call. This kind of service is worth it's weight in a bunch of very heavy things. While leasing, you have more immediate access to improvements in the technology. Upgrading to the newest version of a board may involve no more than trading it in once the new model is available. This should be an advantage, but often isn't because cues recorded on one light board cannot always be played back on a newer version of the same board. This means that all the cues must be hand fed back into the newer machine. Perhaps the major disadvantage of leasing is that it is a on-going expense, not a capital item.

7. *What impact are computerized light boards having?* While the impact on costs can be substantial and welcome, it is the impact on the control of lighting that is the most amazing. The first computer boards were designed and built to solve the problems of large multi-scene preset boards. Remember the discussions about levels not being set right? And cross-faders that got jumpy because almost nobody maintained them? The solutions included the ability to record more than ten cues ahead, the ability to guarantee that the cue you wrote would return to the stage in the form you wrote it, and the ability to operate a smooth cross-fade in real time. With those abilities available, the picture begins to change. Given enough cue storage space to light moment to moment, an assurance that the cues will be repeated as written, and an opportunity to play with the timing, not only eliminates the problems of the preset board, it alters the nature of the way light can interact within a production. Stage light can have a mobility and an accuracy that it hasn't had before. The traditional analogues for lighting have been painting and sculpture, static forms. Add to that the dimension of time and light becomes as dynamic and as expressive as music, and as physically interactive as movement.

8. *Computerized lighting designs are generated by "programming" light boards. Can you give a low-tech explanation of this process?* Programming is the word generally used in the theater to describe the process of loading the level and timing information of the light cues into the light board. For example, "Channel 3 at 50 percent, please. Record in Q 7, time 5." However, it is not programming—it is data entry. Programming, as it is understood in the world of computers, means: "A procedure for solving a problem, including the collection of data, processing that data, and the presentation of results. b. Such a procedure coded for a computer." Programming is instructing the computer to manipulate the data it has been fed. Today's microprocessor-based light board has been programmed at the factory. The boards are set-up to take specific information in a proscribed format, process that information in a predetermined fashion, and generate a limited set of results. Which is to say you can't actually "program" a computer light board, though it would be nice if you could. What you do is "data entry." You enter the level information for each channel and the time the cue happens. This information is recorded in a block of memory under a cue number. You are permitted to alter the information you have entered, but very little else. Capabilities commonplace in home computers, such as the laying out fully customized screens or the global editing of data, are not yet found in the light boards.

9. *Can you justify and describe any cost-effective advantages of computerized lighting systems for dance productions?* Yes. A computer controlled lighting system can effectively cut in half the amount of time spent writing light cues. Or, you might say it effectively doubles the amount of time available to you and your lighting designer to light a dance, to write a lot more cues, or to look at it once more before opening. The amount of time it takes to "write" a light cue has been cut in half because it is no longer necessary to literally write anything down. A hand run board requires that somebody record the information in what amounts to a lighting ledger, the cue sheet. In an even moderately sized set-up, the physical writing down of levels on a piece of paper can take appreciably longer than setting the levels did in the first place.

Now, at the touch of a few buttons, the cue information is stored as electronically encoded information. It can be instantly recalled and rapidly modified. Remember how it used to be when you'd stop a rehearsal, go back and pick it up at the group entrance on stage left? The dancers would take their places and the tape would be wound back and then you'd sit there forever while grumpy people stuffed in that hot box at the back of the room tried to figure out the location of the nobs when they pulled the lever.

10. *What was the first major dance event to use a computerized lighting system?* CHORUS LINE. Without CHORUS LINE we would not have the computerized lighting systems available to us that we have today. More correctly, without the work of Tharon Musser, her technical staff and support from Joe Papp, Michael Bennit, and Robin Wagner, we would probably not have the boards we have.

11. *Who are the leading suppliers of digital lighting systems for dance?* Strand Century's LIGHT PALLETTE would undoubtedly be first. Their light board is the one most prevalently installed in American theaters and the board of choice for most lighting designers. In the rental field, Kliegl's PERFORMER Series is the most readily obtainable. It is portable, easy to learn and dependable. Between the two, there are people who know how to run one or both and how to maintain them. There are a number of other manufacturers as well. A recent issue of THEATER CRAFTS carried ads for control boards built by Electronic Theater Controls, Electro Controls, Dimatronics, Zebedee Products, and Leprecon.

12. *Will computer technology ever eliminate the human element from designing lighting effects for dance?* I certainly hope not.

13. *What ensures that the lighting cues and effects will continue to run smoothly in the event of a power blackout?* Nothing.

14. *Can you describe any lighting disasters during performances which were largely due to electronic control over the lighting design?* Yes I can. These experiences, come from the files of one of America's major ballet companies. If you turn the power switch off on the right side of a Performer, the lights go out, even during a performance. Kicking the power cord out of the wall is equally effective and has the added drama of someone tripping and calling out: "Ooops! Oh, shoot!" Dimmers develop traits and can be perverse about things like neutrals. Breakers get old; and connectors wear out. Computers occasionally do unexpected things, all by themselves. All you have to do to turn out all the lights is unplug one (1) tiny plug or turn off one (1) small switch. The result is a "show stopper"!

15. *In light of all the current computer-aided innovation for dance, do you agree that dancers and choreographers should be more computer literate? If so, how can this be achieved?* If, in the context of lighting, computer literacy means that a choreographer could discuss, in some detail, the "programing mechanics" involved in getting from one cue to the next, no, not necessarily. Most people need no more computer literacy than that needed to use a bank card. When you have uses for a computer, a computer is useful. For tasks that a computer does well, like making endless lists of lekos and fresnels, you can't beat it. But the only computer you need to master is the brain. What really should be explored is the potential these computers represent, the ends to which they are a means. In lighting, the question is one of vision: how do you want to see the light change? Is the pool there when she enters or does it creep up

imperceptibly? Should the lights all fade down to the pool, hold for a moment, and then go out? These are not questions of computer literacy, but of a sensitivity to light in performance.

16. *When you gaze into your computer-lit crystal ball, what can you predict in the future for this area of dance production?* The future appears uncertain. I don't know what technology the computer board manufacturers employ. As far as I know, they don't tell anyone. And I comfort myself by saying that I don't need to know it. Or do I? My impression is that not many people really know what's going on. Today's computer board is just a big black box and a not very bright one at that. Notice that there are no magazines devoted to nifty things you can do with a Performer 2. If there was, it would run one issue. One futuristic way to look at a computer light board is to think of it as a time machine. Another image might be that it is a way to "edit" the light by allowing you to work "blind," that is, without actually seeing the cue up on stage.

17. *Do you have any personal gripes?* This is what I do. I sit here at the Macintosh computer and work. I get up and go down to the Opera House and I sit at the design desk with my headset on and we make light cues on this so-called "computer" light board. It's no computer at all, it's nothing but a big dumb box. So, if computer-based light boards are the solution to the problems of multi-scene preset boards, what's the solution to the problems of computer boards? I wish I could remember the name of the musical. It was on Broadway, about ten years ago. What I remember about it is the sound system. It was notably bad. I remember thinking, "I have a sound system at home, much better than this." For a $40 ticket, I expect more. The light board manufacturers are going to have to face up to the realities of personal computing. In this day and age, it should be possible to enter, manipulate, retrieve, display, and execute the cue information in any fashion I want as easily as one performs spreadsheet, word processing, and data base functions on a personal computer.

18. *What advice do you have for aspiring lighting designers for dance?* Advice? Do a lot of shows. See a lot of dance, all types. Go on the road. Work with a lot of people in as many spaces as possible. Learn something about lekos and dimmers. Look at light and lighting. Look at the world around you. Hang some fresnels, track a few cues. Buy a Macintosh. Watch others light. Design when you can. Ask questions. Talk with choreographers and electricians. Assist. Have fun.

Concluding Comments

As audiences demand technical proficiency in dance productions, whether from the dancers themselves or from the accoutrements of the dance production, special lighting effects and subtleties will more and more reflect this proficiency while at the same time enhance the overall performance. Lighting establishes and sustains the mood of a dance. In the absence of a manipulative environment, dance producers must rely on lighting designs to create optimal conditions for the dance's message. There is every reason to believe that the field of lighting design for dance is still in its infancy. We only have to attend a rock concert or a laserium show to grasp the immediate potential of lighting effects on theatrical performance. Because of their limitless and relatively untapped possibilities due to computer technology, conceiveably lighting designers may actively compete with choreographic designers for visual dominance on stage. Until that day comes, stage lighting and stage dancing should work towards the greatest possible artistic cooperation. A choreographer or artistic director should already be able to demand a most exacting and innovative lighting design to compliment a dance performance. It is now a question of the technology catching up with the ideas and demands of those in the dance field who can use it to enhance their art form.

Figure 14.1
Dramatic lighting during a performance of "Aviary: A Ceremony for Bird People," by the Nikolais Dance Theatre. Photo by Tom Caravaglia

15 The University's Role in the Future of Dance Technology

Judith A. Gray
San Francisco State University
San Francisco, California

As higher educational institutions adapt to more willingly embrace the new technologies, greater collaboration and communication will be demanded of their respective disciplines and constituencies. It has been found repeatedly that the technicians in the computer science departments and laboratories cannot proceed very far without the conceptulists from the arts and humanities. When John Dvorak, technology editor for the *San Francisco Examiner*, was recently asked about the threat of technological Darwinism, he replied that thus far the natural selection process has been in favor of the technologists—"those that know how to sling bits." However, he strongly predicted that the selection pressure will shift towards those with ideas and aesthetic taste. "God knows", he said, "our programmers don't have good aesthetic tastes!"

Conversely, the conceptualists—artists, philosophers, historians, psychologists—are frustrated by their lack of familiarity with the new information technologies. Dance educators, whether they are artists, teachers, or scholars, will be increasingly responsible for providing the conceptual input and direction within the university environment. At the University of California-Irvine, a new Macintosh computer lab has already been challenged by graduate dance students to adapt videographic software to their notation and choreographic needs. It may be that the university's role in the future of dance technology is to ensure a compatible, resourceful working environment: one which will assure the dance researchers and the computer scientists that they have nothing to fear from each other. Indeed, by next century there may be little to distinguish one from the other.

Future Directions

In the future dance teachers, performers, choreographers, students, and audiences may be exposed to or involved in the following endeavors, most of which will be initiated or fostered on university campuses:
1. Interactive compact disk technology for dance;
2. Humanistic (humanoid?) computerized dancer models;
3. Voice input to instruct computers to alter or create dance images;
4. Artificial Intelligence software capable of making choreographic choices;
5. Holographic images of dancers on stage;

Figure 15.1
Dance in the future.

6. Electronic lighting and spatial configurations for dance production;

7. Video sensory systems to accurately record and analyze dance moves;

8. Computer-generated "pseudo dance" which does not involve humans;

9. Sophisticated CAI software for dance instruction and feedback;

10. Home and classroom videocomputers with which armchair choreographers can create their own dances and music scores.

Conclusion

The continued collaboration of dance and computer technology in higher education will likely change the face and perception of dance as an art form. At our universities, dance scholars and artists will have at their fingertips more information and research tools than ever before. Audiences, most of which are developed on college campuses, will be redefined and will come to expect technological innovations and well-engineered dance performances. The relationship between the dance performer and his or her environment will be defined by the imagination and technological literacy of the choreographer. In the dance classroom and studio the teacher's role will be to direct information, rather than transmit it. The need for computer courses and cross-disciplinary studies within the college dance curricula clearly becomes imperative. The more students and teachers of dance there are who are well-informed about computers, the easier it will be to make decisions regarding the aesthetic employment of the new technologies and their inevitable impact on the field of dance in higher education and beyond.